ADVANCE PRAISE FOR

The Enigma of Grief and the Sublime

Johnson mounts a vigorous inquiry into the essential nature and many manifestations of grief and its bond with the sublime, especially in the context of the arts. His analysis of this unique relationship is both deeply personal and profoundly thoughtful. Pickett's trenchant observations on music are integrated into Johnson's premise with care and authority.

— **John David Earnest**, composer, New York, NY

The Enigma of Grief and the Sublime is a unique book in that one must make a commitment to experience what the authors hope to impart. As one who struggled with incomplete mourning after the sudden death of his parents, this book reveals a pathway to natural grief, a far better place. For me, the book's new insights using music, art, and "pairing periods" to accompany patients on the journey to natural grief was a revelation. *The Enigma of Grief and the Sublime* has much to say about aesthetics and philosophy, yes, but for clinicians it will be most useful to those confronting "Persistent Grief Disorder"; it provides new insights into how better to think about it and treat it, and therefore it's essential.

— **Joseph Wujek, MD, FACOG** (retired), Vancouver, WA

I find this book to be illuminating and helpful in understanding grief. I'm particularly drawn to the idea of sublime sadness. This concept resonates to me both artistically and personally. The authors point out numerous artistic examples illustrating the idea. As a jazz musician, I particularly liked the example of "Blue in Green" from the Miles Davis Sextet. I would mention the recording, "Mood" from the Miles Davis Quintet 1965 recording E.S.P. as another example of sublime sadness. Sublime sadness from my personal experience occurred a few days after my mother died. I was playing in an orchestra performing Giuseppe Verdi's "Requiem" and wondering if I was going to make it through the concert under the circumstances. However, I found being part of the performance of this masterpiece was not only painless, it was also very cathartic. This book has helped me to understand that experience much more clearly!

— **David Glenn,** trombonist, composer, Associate Professor of Music (retired), Whitman College

Beautifully written, profound and original essays on the subject of grief, as expressed in art, sculpture, music (classical and jazz), and deeply empathic psychotherapy. The range and specificity of the supporting examples is extraordinary, the cultural literacy astonishing. A wonderful read for mental health practitioners, for those with an interest in aesthetics, and those who are simply intellectually curious. Highly recommended.

— **Franklin G. Maleson, MD,** Training and Supervising Psychoanalyst, Psychoanalytic Center of Philadelphia. Faculty, Sidney Kimmel College of Medicine at Thomas Jefferson University

I have read this book as one recently bereaved, one still in mourning. The book is written with extraordinary empathy and clinically informed insight into the depths and mysteries of grief — and of the heart's and mind's myriad defenses against it. *The Enigma of Grief and the Sublime* gently guides each reader to discover their own path to natural grief. Every reader will find resonant, personally meaningful works of sublime sadness in the wide-ranging examples of how the creative imagination has responded to mourning across the centuries in architecture, painting, poetry, and music. The artistic works depicted and discussed contain, convey, and conjure feelings of primary grief.

Written by authors with deep practice as musicians, a psychotherapist, and a psychiatrist, *The Enigma of Grief and the Sublime* offers consolation, companionship, and illumination to all who mourn and to all who care for the bereaved. This is a book to return to again and again, a book inside which a reader can dwell for many hours, each one of which it will richly repay with comfort, understanding, and a widening of vision — the latter extending the horizon of the reader's own inner landscape.

— **Richard Middleton-Kaplan, PhD,** Director
Academic Support Services, Whitman College

In Memory Of

John Keats

(D. 1821, AGE 25)

and

Franz Schubert

(D. 1828, AGE 31)

He sought to counsel and to calm the despairing man by pointing out to him the man of resignation, and to transform the grief which looks down into the grave by showing it the grief which looks up to the stars.

— Victor Hugo, *Les Misérables*

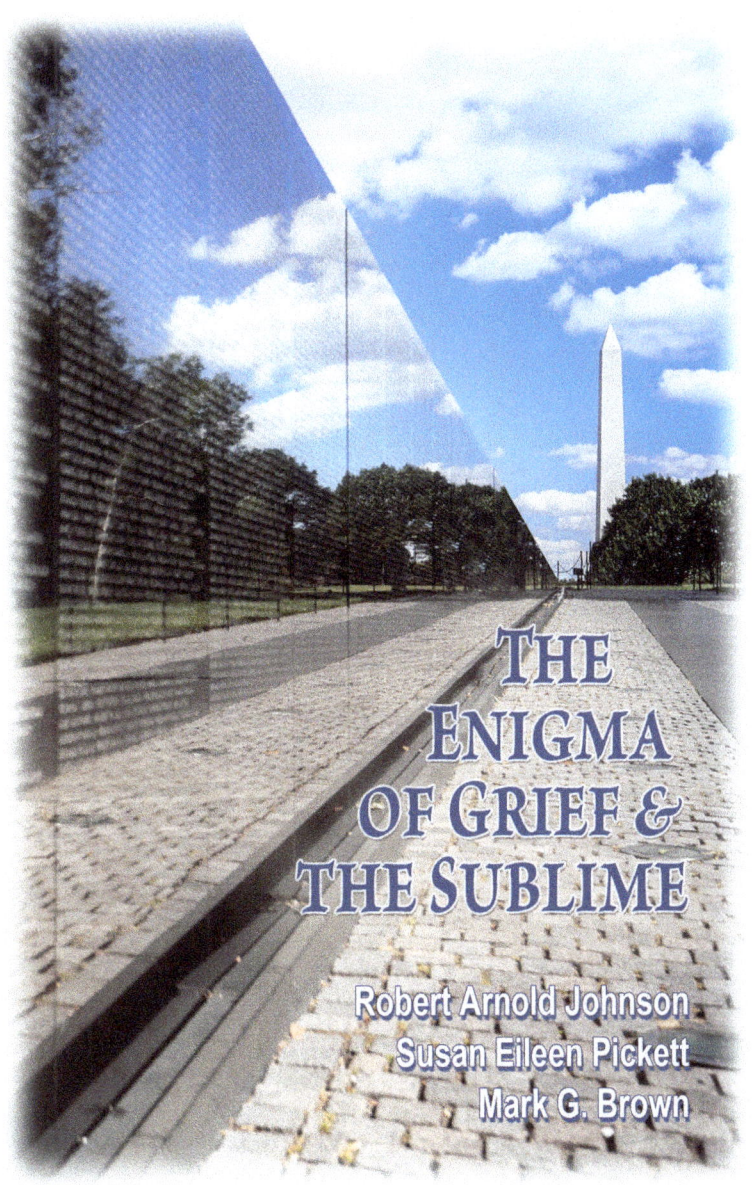

The Enigma of Grief & The Sublime

Robert Arnold Johnson
Susan Eileen Pickett
Mark G. Brown

ROBERT ARNOLD JOHNSON
WALLA WALLA, WA

THE ENIGMA OF GRIEF AND THE SUBLIME

by
Robert Arnold Johnson, Susan Eileen Pickett,
and Mark G. Brown

www.thesublimesadness.com

Copyright © 2025 by Robert Arnold Johnson
Published by the author in Walla Walla, WA
in affiliation with Fearless Literary

No part of this book may be reproduced, distributed, or transmitted in any form or by any means, including photocopying, recording, artificial intelligence tools, or other electronic or mechanical methods, without the prior written permission of the author, except in the case of brief quotations embodied in critical reviews and certain other noncommercial uses permitted by copyright law.

ISBN: 979-8-218-67826-5

LIBRARY OF CONGRESS CONTROL NUMBER:
2025917449

DESIGN, TYPOGRAPHY, AND PRODUCTION
D. Patrick Miller

www.fearlessbooks.com/Literary.html

Contents

Foreword by Samuel Jones 1
Preface by Paul Rotterdam 3
Introduction by Robert Arnold Johnson 5

I   **Art and the Evocation of Natural Grief**
    by Robert Arnold Johnson 25

II   **Evocation of Sublime Sadness:**
    Jazz and Popular Music
    by Mark G. Brown 59

III   **A Work of Art and a Nation's Grief**
    by Robert Arnold Johnson 67

IV   **Musical Structure and Sublime Sadness**
    by Susan Eileen Pickett 77

V   **Art and Easing the Suffering of Loss:**
    In Everyday Life and within Psychotherapy
    by Robert Arnold Johnson 91

VI   **The Oneness of Grief and the Sublime:**
    An Elaboration
    by Robert Arnold Johnson 115

References 127
About the Authors 136
Acknowledgments 138

Foreword

At one time or another, most of us (I am tempted to say, all of us) have looked up into the night sky and wondered about the mystery of the stars and the meaning of life. We instinctively know that there's something deeper going on than just the physics of life, the measurable, quantifiable "facts" of our bodies and our surroundings. Our lives have moments of great exhilaration, but also times when we experience a sense of deep mourning, of intense sadness, especially when facing the loss brought by the death of loved ones.

Robert Arnold Johnson has pondered these things and has given them careful study from several perspectives — that of a physician, a psychiatrist, a novelist, a student of aesthetics, as well as a father, husband, and an academic colleague. This book is the culmination of a lifetime of thought and of sharing the insights he has gleaned from his vast experience. It reflects a remarkable career of service to others and of a search for meaning to it all.

Get ready for some bracing mental calisthenics, however, because you'll find yourself digging into the meaning-beyond-the-meaning of some important everyday concepts. In this day of the astonishing revelations of the James Webb Space Telescope, Johnson and his fellow authors lead us to a deeper understanding and, paradoxically, assurance of the enigma that lies at the very heart of all things. This book will speak to both the lay reader and also to its authors' fellow professionals… an astounding accomplishment in its own right. Hang on to your hat… and your heart. — SAMUEL JONES

Preface

THE SUBLIME is a concept to denote the state of mind created by a phenomenon that exceeds the ordinary, akin to awe and wonder. Sublimity has been woven into philosophical dialectics at least since Platonic idealism, the working of souls in Plotinus, and most of all in the aesthetics of Burke and Immanuel Kant. The basic tenant of the Sublime is its absolute greatness: the infinite in nature, the elements of the divine in art, and the enigma of existence in a distant and sublime Universe. Kant notes that "nature is sublime in all appearances which arouse the idea of infinity," which means that all singular appearances unite into a single intuition about the whole. Individual parts lose their name; perception focuses on totality and "creates an emotional state we call sublime."

In the past two centuries the apperception of a work of art changed from the attention to individual elements and their narrative function into the contemplation of the entirety of the work in an uninterrupted intuition, uninterrupted because no rational thinking about individual elements intermingles in the emotional state of the mind (*Geistesstimmung*) when perceiving the totality of the work. Who would expect that a painting, one that looks like a profane object hanging parallel to the wall, can have the aura of a mysterious icon? Who would expect that a piece of music, like Schubert's String Quintet in C (1828), would make it impossible not to silently cry? Who would expect that a poem would change your position in the world by the revelation of an unexpected truth or an unexpected beauty of language? Who would have imagined that a novel would make you leave home forever in the middle of the night? Who would have expected that the loss of a parent or a dear friend would make you wonder about the enigma of existence and life thereafter?

Of course, it is not expected that one pin down the teleological conditions, let's say, of a painting, the structure of a poem, or the physical circumstances of life which are responsible for feelings we connect with Sublimity. What is sublime can solely be located in the experiencing subject. Sublimity created by the loss of a person cannot be described but only intuited.

We spoke of the perception of a painting being the contemplation of totality rather than the interest in the meaning of singular forms. We also spoke of a sublime experience, a total experience. In *The Enigma of Grief and the Sublime* you will see it is applicable to circumstances of life, particularly to the loss of a person. "Natural grief" turns into extended "calm sadness," an emotion that has infiltrated your whole being without justifying it with the imagination of past experiences. It is a state of being that is sublime in all its manifestations, ubiquitous in every mode of life, and only accessible to understanding when feeling it yourself.

— Paul Rotterdam

Introduction

OUR BOOK'S TITLE appears to imply that a concept of enigma somehow unites the psychological experience of grief and the aesthetic experience of the sublime. Indeed, that will be our claim. Our intentions are two. First is to illustrate what natural grief feels like, and for that we invoke the experience of artworks that convey their participation in the sublime. This purpose has an extension, which is to locate the feeling we mean within the larger context of mourning and to describe how doing so may contribute to the relief of the latter's most distressing features. A second intention is to persuade that our claim is useful for conceptualizing why art is art and how and why the arts therefore inform life, including life as it's reflected on within a session of psychotherapy. We are so ambitious, in other words, as to want to be useful both to philosophy and to psychology, to a theory of aesthetics and to a theory of grief.

How did this book's theme, its claim, arise and with what rationale? For me, it was within the context of providing psychotherapy. I found myself, a psychiatrist for persons sometimes having suffered recent, grievous loss, thinking that the distress I was witness to in the therapy session often was not about, directly at least, the loss itself but about having to experience it, i.e., not the *primary* feeling of loss, but a *secondary* one. Often, I'd recall a video I'd seen once during residency training, one in which the psychologist Leigh McCullough is prompting a patient to tell her more about a mournful feeling he's bearing but having difficulty expressing. In the course of her encouragement, she mentions that there is something "right" about the primary feeling of grief, a feeling instantly discernable if one is paying close attention and is willing and able to hold onto it.[1] In McCullough's book, written with several colleagues, *Treating Affect Phobia*, no mentions of the word "right" appear for the primary feeling of grief, but these excerpts contain the idea of it.

> We refer to it as **sadness/grief** to emphasize the major goal in clinical work — "grief work" — and to distinguish it from emotional pain, an inhibitory form of feeling that often involves maladaptive forms of distress or anguish. (McCullough et al., 20.)

> Each opening to tender feelings brings grief, because experiencing something wonderful for the first time carries the realization of all that was missed, as well as the fear that it may be lost in the future. (McCullough et al., 243.)

> If grief can be borne, then the tears that come with tenderness will be experienced as more relieving than punishing. (McCullough et al., 280.)

My reflections on the idea of rightness within the feeling of grief so defined, what in this book we will call variously *intrinsic, innate, primary, natural,* or *essential* grief — the sad feeling that's primary within the experience of loss itself — I coupled with another exercise, that of an intensely focused examination of my own feelings connected with personal experiences of loss. And I compared at the same time that conclusion with the result of focused examination of my feelings as I sat with patients who had themselves experienced losses. Three things in particular came forward.

One, my own feeling during empathic listening to *myself* (rehearsing in my mind a personal loss) matched my feeling during empathic listening *to a patient* (rehearsing her loss). Two, what the patient did (or could) express then, during the early sessions, often did not match what I, the listener, felt, but it came to do so weeks or months later. In short, the patient's feeling of calm, primary sadness had been present all along yet out of her awareness until such time that it could be granted a presence there. It was a feeling, I began to think, that she transmitted unwittingly to an empathic listener, but to which in her own mind she was numb until she could grant herself sufficient empathy.

I'll put off taking up the third matter this exercise brought forward that I might say a bit more first about this specific viewpoint on intrinsic grief. It took origin, as described in the preceding paragraphs, from the work of McCullough and her colleagues. If my personal experience serves as a model, it becomes a conviction, and a useful one, for setting a goal for psychotherapy of those whose experience of loss is so distressingly anguished their daily functioning is impaired.

Yes, it does differ, in detail and in emphasis, from the five-stage viewpoint on grief famously elaborated in the works of Elisabeth Kübler-Ross.[2] The good her works have done to bring us face-to-face, unabashedly and unashamedly, with grieving is undeniable.[3] Yet, to my mind, none of the five stages quite fits what we want the word grief to point to — natural grief, i.e., calm sadness — though we see some examples of just that within the cases Kübler-Ross presents and the poetic fragments she includes. The stages, I believe, are best conceived as defenses against natural grief. Kübler-Ross herself acknowledged as much,[4] but seemed to think the language of defense too technical for the readership she wished to address.

This seemingly subtle reregister in language, however, has consequences. Substituting stages for defenses as explicative for the emotions surrounding (and obscuring) grief tempts the presumption, fully apparent in her later work with David Kessler, that each stage, or at least several, must be borne, lived through — that each or several are, in fact, necessary for successful grieving. Clinical practice does not, in my opinion, bear this out. Kübler-Ross's first work on grief was published more than a half-century ago; I am not its first critic, to understate the matter considerably.[5] Some persons come to calm sadness very early, even as their first emotion of loss. Others work through just one defense, anger, say, before acknowledging the calm sadness that anger has hidden earlier from their awareness. Others work through both denial and anger in succession, or vice versa.

And I find that clinical depression within the course of mourning is just that: it should be treated as depression is treated rather than presumed to be a stage of something. Otherwise, it impedes a natural motion of the mind toward its primary end: intrinsic, natural grief — calm sadness. In short, positing that conscious perception of, and appreciation for, calm sadness is the goal of treatment for persons finding themselves disabled by mourning prescribes a more focused structure for the treatment itself — more than if it is founded on presumptively necessary stages. [6]

Sigmund Freud's demarcation of reactions to loss have been succinctly summarized by Salman Akhtar[7] as sadness (the person or object lost was "deeply loved" but self-definition remains whole), anxiety (the loss threatens the maintenance of self-integration), and mental pain (*Seelenschmerz* — the loss is the mental equivalent of amputation of a body part).

The latter two on Freud's list, I'd point out, may each be considered a defense against self-fragmentation and the first corresponds to natural grief. Newer formulations for grief than Kübler-Ross's are currently in ascendency;[8] they base themselves on attachment theory, disrupted meaning-making, and related constructs (Chapter V) and are proposed by clinical researchers especially concerned with prolonged, pronounced, and impairing distress following loss[9] — a condition so extreme as to now have gained recognition as a mental disorder, an illness, in DSM-5-TR,[10] perhaps affecting as many as ten percent of bereaved persons.

I do find the notion of grief-in-stages insinuated to a varying degree within some of these constructs and the clinical recommendations that follow them. They each define grief as, or imply that it is, the amalgam of affects (emotions) and behaviors that I herein have labeled defenses; in none can I find an affect defined, or even spoken of,[11] that promotes or parallels the cognitive integration each sees as, eventually, a relief to the suffering that has preceded it. In Chapter V, I will have further commentary.

If, as we claim here, the primary motion of the mind in confronting loss is toward the affect of natural grief — adaptive, calm sadness — why would that same mind mount defenses against its own nature? In the language of Sigmund Freud and Salman Akhtar we'd answer this way: an attempt to remain whole under the duress of loss. Is such a language coherent when it comes to conceptualizing the various "maladaptive" emotions that so often come forward during mourning?

My answer is multipartite. First, I do believe the language of defense is coherent in this setting. Second, I'd postulate that the unconscious motive for defense, designed in the face of loss to impede progress toward an otherwise natural goal of the mind, is to avoid the cost of that goal's accommodation. Third, I'd point out that the final book of Kübler-Ross, coauthored with Kessler, is especially helpful on this second point: the experience of loss changes us, creates a wound within our sense of who we are[12] — a wound we are tempted to erase instantly, however illusory that erasure is, rather than to heal.

True, the calm of primary sadness — the rightness within it — soothes the wound like a salve; the more innate grief we feel, the more our wounded self, our who-ness, adjusts, adapts, and heals. But to experience the presence and therefore the benefit of natural grief, we must implicitly acknowledge and bear two things: the loss itself (loss as loss) and a disruption within the makeup of who we are, a new uncertainty, an angst, within our selfness. Hence these common defenses. Nobody I know of provides a better description of working through them to arrive at natural grief than does the famous author C. S. Lewis, recounting his personal experience after the death of his spouse.[13]

Who we are has an enigmatic core,[14] meaning that it cannot be captured in problem-centered language. A problem is something begging for solution; once solved, it disappears. Enigma isn't solvable, because it is not a problem.[15] Reflection deepens it;[16] it becomes revealed as enigma, known as such, in the moment it is grasped as a reveal of possibility, arising, often as a surprise, from one's realization that a prior presumption has just been exposed for what it is: a presumption. In the case of confronting the distress of loss, one presumes the loss as a limiting or restricting condition for *who* one is. But is it? Once grasped, intuitively or by reflection, as enigma, I can ask these questions, among others: Who will I now become? Must I presume that who I will become, now that I bear this loss, is limited? Or is it that I will be changed? Does change in itself imply limitation? Isn't it possible, even likely, that who I am will be deepened by my coming to grips with the experience of loss and thereby an experience of reality?

Natural, primary grief, then, as we are defining it here, is the sadness appropriate to loss. Yet simultaneously it's the rightness appropriate to comprehending, about oneself, enigma for what it is. It is, in short, the affective parallel for the enigma of who we are in confronting loss.

Not that all enigma is about loss. Or is it? Well, consider the enigma of *who*. When I know someone, I recognize her; I provide an answer, if asked, to "Who is she?" She is *who* she is, not *what* she is. Which means neither I nor anyone can possess her; she has but one owner: herself.[17] Someone attempting, or presuming, to own her sees her as *what*, not as *who*. And in the impossibility of my owning her, I feel, however unconsciously, a form of loss; she is something, partially yet essentially, denied to me, I cannot wholly *have* her. But the feeling I experience in knowing who she is — that feeling is not completed by the fact of loss; there is, *pari passu*, so often a larger gain: the joy (or fear, among other possibilities — it all depends, of course) of knowing her as herself, say a companion, a friend, a confidant, an ally. If my experience of who she is makes me fearful — let's say I take her to be predatory, whatever else she is — then I am on my guard; at the least I have the confidence thereby provided — I am as capable as a steward of my security as my circumstance can allow. But before I lose my point, let me reclaim it: the enigma of *who* contains, however subtly, some small loss for any others who know me; my gain through being who I am, in other words, is your loss in knowing that *I* am (who I am). To make this assertion, I need not believe that loss comprises the whole measure of enigma that a who embeds within itself.

I am tempted to say this much, though: that loss, by its nature, any loss, presents an enigma, and one easiest to understand from its flip side, possession. What does it mean to possess something, anything? Whatever a complete answer to this question would look like, we may see that it must hold, at a minimum, this: to think (or feel or intuit) that you *possess* something, including yourself, or that someone else does, implies a possessing self, a possessor. Moreover, a self itself (*who*), is an act of self-possession, a state of owning one's thoughts, emotions, sensations, and experiences (experiences of fact, will, accomplishment, deception, failure, and, yes, one's body[18]). And then there's the fact that if loss is that of a person, one never was in possession of that person anyhow (see above). Though some will decry what I've done here as circuitous, I descry it as pointing toward enigma. Possession, when the word is used beyond the most primitive sense of containing, is enigmatic.[19] And so, therefore, is its counterpart: loss. I'll revise now a locution I used earlier: grief is the affective parallel for the enigma of yourself confronting the enigma of your loss — enigma doubly charged.

If I've been persuasive, all loss is enigmatic. Is the reverse true? Is all enigma a form of loss? Perhaps. Consider examples: First, the big bang. How may one speak of time or cause before there's a universe within which either might exist? Yet we have reasonable evidence the big bang happened! Just how does something "happen" in or from a timeless nowhere? We may postulate: God or gods; a Higgs-like field; or just one bang within a succession of bangs.[20] But whence came him/her/them/physical event or field?

The ancient Greeks, as is well known, supposed one set of gods giving way to another — a theistic progression. But of course, such postulates raise the question: how may we locate the very first, the prime, mover? And how may we expect to know or learn the origin of something we ourselves are contained within, i.e., to comprehend as if from beyond our world(s) looking in?[21] How do we comprehend as much as we do anyway, without presuming that something like "mind" — immaterial, therefore disembodied — exists and has existed beyond ourselves, permeating everywhere?[22]

One hypothesis has been that the "whatness" of the cosmos, whether singular or plural, whether or not it contains bangs, is infinite — no beginning, no end. Yet what is meant by the word *infinite* in such a context? How might I understand such a thing? Perhaps, and here is the position I favor, we will be satisfied best by understanding "whence," when it comes to a cosmos, as pointing toward enigma rather than problem. Not, "There is no whence!" Not, "Of course there is! Science must never give up!" But this: "The whence for a cosmos is enigmatic."[23] The possibility that time and space may not come first within a cosmos, but emerge from a reality even more fundamental,[24] only heightens the enigma of its "whence."

Does my suggestion too much favor people of religious faith? A deity feels no obligation to explain herself, being enigmatic by definition. Well, it provides to religious faith a position, so far as enigma is concerned, as reasonable as any other, but only so long as the bearers of the faith are true, and remain so, to this conception: enigma is the foundation of faith itself. That is, so long as they see faith and its content as providing a name for the enigma-of-all. Once it is seen instead as solving the problem of "whence," they are working outside my suggestion, in which case I may not be charged with favoring them.[25] And I am uncertain what "too much favor" would mean in such a question anyhow. Now, does the enigma of a cosmos, whether it bears a name, via faith, or not, provoke some sense of loss in those who perceive it? Yes. I must let go of the security a solution would hold for me, that vague sense of control — its fume of certainty — residing within my *really* knowing how or why.

Another example: Some persons have the mental experience of witnessing an event — something that they are not, or were not, actually a witness to, yet did take place or has in the world somewhere, sometime. Many variations on this kind of experience are reported, which may, it seems, constitute in some a talent, a capacity, one that can be cultivated even. And the documentation for such experiences appears incontrovertible.[26] Such documentation may be studied via scientific method and has been — perhaps even some neurologic correlate will prove possible to "see" by means of brain imaging — but it seems impossible to *explain* them scientifically, to explain just how information from an event distant in time, place, or both would arrive as an experience of it to the capable subject.

Mourning about someone dying or someone recently deceased is sometimes punctuated by uncanny experiences of this sort.[27] Time will tell, yet perhaps such things will forever best be viewed as enigmatic. Does a decision to do so provoke the feeling of loss? Yes, for the same reason given for the enigma that is embedded within the existence of a cosmos.

Still other examples are provided by various versions of the greatest of existential dilemmas. Does my life, or any life, matter? Are we all simply a vehicle for *who*-ness on its way to death? A view that such questions are exemplary for several formulations of enigma seems reasonable, at the least. I may watch my mind go to the possibilities inherent within different ways of answering them. And which of those seems most suitable for me now? Why? I am immersed thereby in a state of wonder, "the very beginning of philosophy,"[28] a deep reflection on the enigmatic. And is a feeling of loss provoked by such a stance? Most surely: again, for the same reason given for the enigma that is embedded within the existence of a cosmos.

Or consider the enigmatic possessed within every work of art. We will have much more to say and show in this regard, but one way to become quickly immersed, even submerged, within the notion is to read Calvin Tomkins on the work of the American artist David Hammons.[29] Here is one excerpt: "Beauty and ugliness cohabit in these works, enhancing and negating each other, forcing us to confront the beauty in ugliness, and vice-versa." Or read Paul Rotterdam's collection of his own writings on the role and nature of feeling in looking at art and in creating it.[30] Or this, by artist and critic Fairfield Porter:[31] "Art permits you to accept illogical immediacy, and in doing so releases you from chasing after the distant and ideal. When this occurs, the effect is exalting."

An explication for our theme has gained some ground. Natural grief, though we have yet to illustrate the feeling of it, has been defined. It is always about loss, whether great or small. Loss is enigmatic (which subtracts not a whit from its reality), as is *who-*anyone-is suffering the loss (which subtracts not a whit from the reality of *who* one is). Enigma itself, once acknowledged, is loss, in part. The calm sadness of primary grief, borne repeatedly over time, heals the distressing disruption within who is experiencing it as she bears the loss that caused it. Innate grief compels an intuition of rightness about bearing it. But is *right* the last word on the property within grief that McCullough believed was primary, essential, about it?

Still another thing came forward within my observational exercises described earlier. There was a feeling of the sublime evoked by, contained within, the experience of innate grief as I've defined it here — embedded securely within its sadness. And that portion of the feeling has a powerful consequence: it makes sitting with it — one's own primary grief or another's — effortless. Yes, practice — enough that the sitting takes on a degree of familiarity — helps. We are drawn to people grieving![32] The intuition that the word *sublime* more exactly specifies an aspect of natural grief, its prosocial quality, than was accomplished by the word rightness is strengthened, for me at least, by a particularly moving section within Ernest Becker's *The Denial of Death*.[33] And several passages applying or implying the word sublime for expressing the nature of grief appear within Victor Hugo's *Les Misérables*; we make one such an epigraph for this book, but we might have chosen another for the same purpose.

Tempting indeed, then, to think that a principle within the "whence" of primary grief is overtly biologic.[34] That principle might be stated like this: natural grief is an evolved affect, one that draws in the support and sustenance of a community, large or small, at a time its assistance is, literally, vital; in short, primary grief conveys an increment in likelihood that a wounded and vulnerable victim of loss will survive — a practical, material result flowing out of sublime sadness.[35] In Chapter VI, we will take up further literary, philosophical, and psychological supports we see for conceiving of the sublime as we do and for claiming that it and sadness are within the same experience.

— ROBERT ARNOLD JOHNSON

NOTES

1. I have not succeeded in retrieving a copy of that video. McCullough has since died.
2. Kübler-Ross, *On Death and Dying*. Kübler-Ross and Kessler, *On Grief and Grieving*.
3. The five stages are now even musically described in an opera! (See Batycka, "Defying the Odds.") This is not to imply that their author, Kübler-Ross, is the first ever to imagine that mourning takes place in stages; the idea is presented by John Bowlby, too, as early as 1961 (see Bowlby, *Loss*, 85), although he uses the term phases in place of stages, and at the

same time, he makes clear the identity and nature of the defenses contained within the phases. An admirably concise history of conceiving mourning as an unfolding in stages is presented by John Wilson in *Supporting People through Loss and Grief*, see especially 81-2.
4. Kübler-Ross, *On Death and Dying*, 138. Some writers, I'm thinking mainly of Rachel Gibbons ("The mourning process and its importance in mental illness..." 80-8), are comfortable with treating the word "stage" as a near-synonym with "defense," but, as I hope to make clear, I'm not. I do highly recommend, however, Gibbons's paper, which argues that all mental illness may be viewed a result of adaptation to loss, i.e., a form of mourning, though she has no intention of denying genetic and other biologic factors their due.
5. See, for example, Dennis, "The Grief River," 105.
6. Judaism's sequential ritual of mourning is instructive here. The sequence is: *aninut*, immediate distress of loss (signified by wearing a torn garment), between death of the loved one and burial; *shivah*, the seven-day period commencing the day of burial wherein the bereaved family stays at home in its "low" state while friends and relatives bring food, tidy the family's home, and condole with its members if that gesture is welcome; *sheloshim* completes a thirty-day period (counting *shivah*) wherein the mourners return to work but avoid public places of entertainment; *shnat ha-evel,* the remainder of the first year after burial in which the mourners are to be active in normal life except for saying the Mourner's Kaddish (a thirteen-line prayer in Aramaic from the 13th century celebrating God) daily — by implication, mourners are certifying their faith despite the loss they have had to suffer. One may be tempted to look on the sequence as evidence that the Jewish faithful believe that mourning requires stages (see Bowlby, *Loss*, 130). But an equally tempting interpretation is to presume that the goal is to compel as soon as is humane a casting aside of defenses, hence a transition to natural grief earlier than it might have happened otherwise.
7. See Akhtar's *In Short*, 38.
8. See Neimeyer and Thompson, "Meaning Making," 3–6.
9. Maciejewski and Prigerson, "Prolonged, But Not Complicated, Grief."
10. *Diagnostic and Statistical Manual of Mental Disorders,* 5th ed., text revision.
11. I may be accused of overstatement here. In John Bowlby's celebrated *Loss*, for example, a source widely admired among contemporary

clinician-scholars, there is this brief passage about children bearing the loss of a parent: "whereas for others tears brought relief" (Bowlby, *Loss*, 286), which might imply the affect I quote McCullough as describing; at other times, Bowlby uses the word sorrow in a seemingly tender way. Yet he does not define this affect, if that is what he means to describe in the passage I quote, as the essence of grief within the process of mourning, thereby constituting the goal toward which that process tends.

12. See, in this regard: Neimeyer and Cacciatore, "Developmental Theory of Grief"; M. Katherine Shear, "Grief Is a Form of Love"; Salman Akhtar, *Three Faces of Mourning*, 100–102.
13. Lewis, *A Grief Observed*.
14. Johnson and Davis, *Story by Story*, esp. Davis's chap. 2, "Philosopher: Reading Zack's Story". See also Butler, *Giving an Account*, esp. 82–83, Cavell, "Finding Words," 5, and Calasso, *The Marriage*, 343-344. Note: brilliant, and usefully provocative, as I find several literary and cultural theorists of recent decades, in this work a theoretical debate about the real or fictional status of the *self* itself (for example, see Culler, *Literary Theory*, 110–20) will be presumed to be settled thus: a concept of *self* is indispensable for grappling conceptually with the very real experiences of grief and of the sublime.
15. A variant on this statement might be to this effect: enigma embodies something "inexpressible," meaning it resists language-as-description, at least direct description; its relationship to language is via connotation, not denotation — is evocative, not descriptive. (The composer John David Earnest has brought to my attention here that the English enigma derives from the Greek verb *ainissesthai*, meaning *to speak allusively*.) For especially rich statements of this idea, see: Gadamer, *The Relevance of the Beautiful and Other Essays*, 21; and the artist Paul Rotterdam's *Wild Vegetation*, 177.
16. This aspect of the enigmatic about the self is writ bold when it becomes itself the point of a story, even (or especially) if parodied. See James Wood's piece on the Catherine Lacey novel *Pew* (Wood, "Catherine Lacey and the Art of Enigma").
17. This does not imply that who she is originates autonomously, in a kind of parthenogenesis. She blossoms into herself *among others*, most often within a family to begin with, a family of *language-speakers*, and continues to exist and grow (or stagnate, even regress) in her identity,

most especially via its moral dimension, within what Charles Taylor calls "webs of interlocution" (Taylor, *Sources of the Self*, 36) and Thomas Alderson Davis calls "a community of listeners" (Johnson and Davis, "Philosopher: Reading Zack's Story," chap. 2 in *Story by Story*). As Taylor puts it, "one cannot be a self on one's own" (Taylor, 36). To be clear, my position herein is that *who* and derivatives, such as *free will*, are features of experience, not features of, nor definable from, stuff(s), materials, "substances," and a statement attributed to Francis Crick, "Who you are is nothing but a pack of neurons," (Sapolsky, *Determined*, 247), obviously posits a position quite to the contrary, one that I will not pursue.

18. We commonly speak of our bodies as "ours," though the expression itself is enigmatic. Consider this comment by Gabriel Marcel: "I cannot validly say 'I and my body'" (Marcel, *Being and Having*, 117). Still, how to speak otherwise? A problem (yes, pun intended). Marcel was well aware of the "problem" he introduced: this book and others he wrote are marvelous ruminations on the matters of possessing and losing, problem and mystery, and still other aspects of the enigmatic in philosophy.
19. Jean-Paul Sartre put it this way: "the ambiguity of the idea of possession" (Sartre, *Baudelaire*, 68–69).
20. Penrose, *Big Bang*.
21. I cannot resist quoting here from Meghan O'Gieblyn's *God Human Animal Machine* (123-124). "There is no Archimedian point, no purely objective vista that allows us to transcend our human interests and see the world from above, as we once imagined it appeared to God… It was Max Planck, the physicist who struggled more than any other pioneer of quantum theory to accept the loss of a purely objective worldview, who acknowledged that the central problems of physics have always been reflexive. 'Science cannot solve the ultimate mystery of nature,' he wrote in 1932. 'And that is because, in the last analysis, we ourselves are part of nature and therefore part of the mystery that we are trying to solve.'"
22. Nagel, *Mind and Cosmos*.
23. My suggestion here is hardly original. It is explicit, just for example, within the "mysteries" that circulated in ancient Greece pertinent to beginnings. See Roberto Calasso's *The Marriage of…*, esp. 197-207.
24. Adam Becker, "Origins of Space and Time."

25. This is written tongue-in-cheek as a reply to Freud, who in *Civilization and Its Discontents* (10–15) discusses the place of religion in human affairs and the force of the enigmatic within it. His commentary has a dismissive slant that seems to betray some limitation for appreciating, therefore acknowledging, or even perceiving, enigma. Freud's was a brilliant mind, unquestionably, but brilliance is not all of a kind. What Freud specifically is denying is ever having experienced himself an "oceanic" feeling or comprehension, a unity of all things — something like the mind-pervades-all conclusion that Thomas Nagel came to by logical means (Nagel, *Mind and Cosmos*), but arrived at instead via intuition, sudden or otherwise. However it's arrived at, I will cite it as exemplary of an experience of existential enigma generally, whether Plotinus's absolute "Good" (Cooper, *Aesthetics: The Classic Readings*, 64); Chinese artist Shih-t'ao's "The One" (Cooper, 72); Dante's vision of God at the culmination, the transcendent apogee, of his *Divine Comedy*; the "limitlessness" in Kant's commentary on the sublime (*Critique of Judgment*, loc. 1208 of 5002); the "Emptiness" of Japanese philosopher Nishitani Keiji (see Unno, Religious Philosophy); or many other examples of an ineffable feeling provoked by art or religious experience (Scruton, "Music and the Transcendental," chap. 4 in *Music as an Art*).
26. Mayer, *Extraordinary Knowing*.
27. Morningstar, "Visual Experiences," "Auditory Experiences," "Kinesthetic Awareness," and "Dreams," chap. 3–6 in *Honoring the Mystery*. Luzzi, *In a Dark Wood*, 108–9.
28. See Pieper, *Leisure*, 98–116, an extraordinary discourse on the interrelationships of wonder, philosophy, and enigma.
29. Tomkins, "The Enchanter."
30. Rotterdam, *Wild Vegetation*. Just for example, one with consummate husbandry: "We look at art to look at artists," 205.
31. Porter, *Art in Its Own Terms*, 106.
32. This is true when grief is the primary kind. The defenses so often in the way of natural grief, however, are not attractive: we are repulsed by them; we put up with them within ourselves or as we bear witness to them in others, with effort or anguish (identification), because we believe it our duty to do so or because we see no alternative. Never forget, though, that such defenses are unconsciously motivated; a person caught up in them is unaware of their underlying motivation and cannot there-

fore be "culpable" for them. Help for such a person must arise out of kindness, not accusation! Often enough, an expression of a defensive affect, such as anguish, is so poignant it's as if the sufferer is, unconsciously, an artist; or sometimes the sufferer *is* an artist (see Hirsch, *Gabriel*). In these instances, the sublime, an aspect of natural grief, is evoked within the attentive witness (see Chap. I). And in addition, as I've declared above about my own experience as a therapist, an attentive witness who lets the sufferer's defensive affect be, without identifying with it, will often begin to feel the innate grief that underlies it.

33. Becker, *Denial of Death*, 150–52.
34. The observation that nonhuman animals that exhibit mourning-like behaviors are those that are most social does nothing, of course, to contradict this sentence. See, for example, King, "Orca's Sorrow," 32–35.
35. Consider this statement from the sociologist and hospice physician Nicholas Christakis: "Death and grief unite us like nothing else" (Christakis, *Blueprint*, xvii). Or if that sentence seems too blunt, consider the sublime sadness one feels reading even a summary, most especially if one has once seen the play staged, of Sophocles's *Antigone* (e.g., Grant, *Classical Greeks*, 111–12). Natural grief is silently transmitted to a sensitive witness and, furthermore, to a witness of the witness — see Anthony Lane's beautiful account of Jane Austen's final months (Lane, "Last Laugh"). I wish we had clear evidence about the origin and development, if development is required, of essential grief — sublime sadness — in children, but if such exists, I have not yet located it. Melvin Konner's magisterial *The Evolution of Childhood*, has only this, really, to say about all positive emotions (not to speak of aesthetic feeling generally, let alone the sublime): that they "grade into one another; they do not fully overlap, but they are difficult to define" (Konner, 512–13). We have studies of aesthetic judgment by children (see, for example, Housen and Yenawine, *Visual Thinking Strategies*; Almeida-Rocha, Peixoto, and Neves Jesus, "Aesthetic Development in Children"; and Clarke, "Psychology of Music"), but these take on cognitions or preferences; I am unable to tell how or whether the child feels beauty or the sublime — a specifically aesthetic feeling — i.e., the phenomenology of it. Of course, the range of available descriptive language for feeling is of considerable importance in making anything like complete judgments about children and affect. The first experience of sublime sadness I'm able to identify in my own past

took place at age eight, when an older friend, a teenager much beloved within our family for having rescued my next younger brother from drowning, was killed a week later on a local roadway. My first experiences of the sublime in relation to artworks I'd date to ages ten to fourteen. To be clear, our concept of "aesthetic feeling," hardly original to us, refers to pleasurable (positive) affect pertinent alone to the experience of beauty and not to another pleasure, such as the joy of movement, the joy of love, the joy of observing another's pleasure, the joy of accomplishment, or the satisfaction of an appetitive drive.

CHAPTER I

Art and the Evocation of Natural Grief

ROBERT ARNOLD JOHNSON

WHAT DOES primary, natural grief, sublime sadness, feel like? One way to demonstrate would be to evoke the experience of loss in a straightforward way, say by telling a story about it. The limitation in such a method is that its author does not have a way of controlling his reader's response: will she feel innate grief or one or more of the several defenses against it? There's no telling in advance. So I will proceed in reverse. I'll present a piece of art that I believe evokes the sublime and then ask the reader to reflect on the similarity of that affect, now that he is mindful of it, with a special form of sadness, one that he might locate in his own memory of mourning loss in the past (although he may not have, at the time, thought of it as grief).

The artworks I present are simply some among the many, many I find evocative of the sublime; they may or may not contain a depiction of grief. Their depiction is not their point, from our standpoint; their evocation is.[1] That's why instrumental music may be just as sublime as sad opera or theater or cinema, why an abstract painting or sculpture may be just as effective for a setting of sublime sadness as Goya's painting of execution by firing-squad or Picasso's Guernica. Is there something wrong with you if you look at one of the pieces herein and don't get it? No. We're none of us receptive at each and every moment to "getting it." I am confident, though, that you will get at least one of the pieces. And one is enough. You will know in that moment what I mean by *sublime sadness.*

On another reading (listening, viewing), when your mind is right for it (sometimes the reason will be apparent to you but more often a mystery, if you're like me), you will find yourself feeling the sublime about one or more of the pieces that had been unmoving the first time around. Once you have the feeling in your storehouse of experience and have identified it as such, you will find it not only in many works of art you've come to admire, or discover you can admire, but also within your experience of the world around you, both natural and social. And those occasions will take on a new value, most especially the value and wonder of being alive for them, sad as they may be.

The text will be in brief passages, which for the most part are prompts to something elaborated in more detail in the Introduction or in Chapter VI. The creator of each piece will be identified, when known to me; if the piece bears a title, it will be provided, along with its location where applicable. For musical pieces, choose the streaming service of your preference: Apple Music, SoundCloud, Spotify, YouTube Music, and Amazon Music are just some examples wherein each is available. I have provided a suggestion for a recording in each instance (and for Chapter IV, this recording will correspond to the times specified within the pieces selected for discussion); this is a suggestion only: do not feel obligated to use it — choose another performance and other performers should that be most convenient, given the choices provided by your streaming service. If you choose the suggestion I have made, you may make use of this book's website (*www.thesublimesadness.com*) to access its live hyperlink. The chapter from here forward can easily take up to three hours or more, which need not happen within a single sitting, of course. At least once through, though, read every word, ponder each photograph, listen to every note, whether that requires one extended session or a half-dozen briefer ones.

In the case of vocal music sung in a foreign language, whether opera or song, I purposely do not provide an English text for the words, nor do I relate (in the case of opera) the story. With one exception (where I will comment), the music must itself elicit the sense of sublime sadness, just as instrumental music or an abstract work of visual art might do. I present no summary at the chapter's end. The pieces must persuade, on their own. One cannot be bullied into feeling grief (which does not imply that suggestions and seductions are of no help). This chapter is designed to provide a space, a kind of contemplative sanctuary, in which that happening takes place, one that is more immersive than it is discursive.[2]

PIECE 1.1. Vincenzo Bellini, "Casta diva," from his opera *Norma*, first performed in 1831. Recording: *Diva: The Very Best* *of Anna Netrebko,* Deutsche Grammophon, 2018. Performed by soprano Anna Netrebko and the SWR Symphony Orchestra, conducted by Marco Armiliato.

> Natural grief is sublime sadness. It is always about loss, whether absolute or relative. It draws us to the one bearing it; we want to witness and to help. Eyes are wet, perhaps — maybe tears trickle — but are not heavily lachrymose. Innate grief, so defined, does not torment. Our job as witnesses is simply to sit by in loving presence; we need say nothing at all. Natural grief is highly prosocial, highly adaptive. It asks nothing of us except empathic silence, which it draws from us wordlessly. Its witness is likely to become a steadfast helper, if needed.

PIECE 1.2. Bob Dylan, "Don't Think Twice, It's All Right." Recording: *Bob Dylan's Greatest Hits Volume II,* Columbia, 1971. Performed by Bob Dylan.

> Conventionally considered a song, this work evokes sublime sadness as much, perhaps more, by Dylan's vocalized poetic force as by its musical means. *See Chapter IV.*

PIECE 1.3. Raphael, *Madonna del Granduca,* 1504, Pitti Palace, Florence, Italy, oil on wood, 84 56 cm. Photograph courtesy of Web Gallery of Art.

> Primary grief is calm and sad, whereas serenity is calm, not sad. The calm in this picture is indisputable. Is its Madonna serene or is she sad? Or is she both? Is both

even possible? Or is she serene (depiction) and you're sad (evocation)? Or may the viewer's feeling vacillate, an aspect of the work's magnificence?

PIECE 1.4. Pablo Picasso, *Science and Charity*, Barcelona, [January-April] 1897. Oil on canvas, 197.5 x 250 cm. Museu Picasso, Barcelona. Gift of Pablo Picasso, 1970. MPB 110.046. Museu Picasso, Barcelona. Photo: Fotogasull. ©2025 Estate of Pablo Picasso / Artists Rights Society (ARS), New York, NY.

Here grief is what's indisputable, because natural grief is depicted within the picture — the artist likely seeking to evoke it. Much more often, I believe, an artist works in obedience to a feeling, one that goes unnamed, because its naming is unconscious and unneeded; the artist simply insists the work must feel "right" as it proceeds. T. S. Eliot once gave overt expression to this phenomenon when he responded to a published review about one of his poems with the comment that, at last, he knew what it meant.[3] He was serious.

PIECE 1.5. Ludwig van Beethoven, Violin Concerto in D Major, op. 61, second movement (Larghetto), first performed in 1806. Recording: *Beethoven Violin Concerto/Violin Romances Nos. 1 and 2,* Philips Classics, 1986. Performed by violinist Henryk Szeryng and the Royal Concertgebouw Orchestra, Amsterdam, conducted by Bernard Haitink. (If the music goes on much after 9:30, you may stop, because the merge with the third movement does not contain a pause.)

PIECE 1.6. Mark Strand (1934–2014), "Provisional Eternity" from ALMOST INVISIBLE: POEMS by Mark Strand, copyright 2012 by Mark Strand. Used by permission of Alfred A. Knopf, an imprint of the Knopf Doubleday Publishing Group, a division of Penguin Random House LLC. All rights reserved.

> A man and a woman lay in bed. "Just one more time," said the man, "Just one more time." "Why do you keep saying that?" said the woman. "Because I never want it to end," said the man. "What don't you want to end?" said the woman. "This," said the man, "this never wanting it to end."

PIECE 1.7. Sergei Rachmaninov, Romance/Ballade, op. 1, no. 5, in A Major, ca. 1890. Recording: *Rachmaninov: Music for Cello and Piano,* Alto Recordings, 2011. Performed by cellist Marina Tarasova and pianist Alexander Poleshaev.

Pieces 1.5 and 1.7 show that "grief music" need not be written in a minor key. (Much more will be said about how innate grief becomes inscribed into musical structure in Chapter IV.)

PIECE 1.8. Clara Schumann, Romanze no. 1, from Drei Romanzen, op. 22, 1853. Recording: *Clara Schumann: Piano Concerto, Piano Trio, Three Romances,* Tudor, 2005. Performed by violinist Joseph Silverstein and pianist Veronica Jochum.

PIECE 1.9. "Barbara Allen," ca. 1666 (first mention in print), a traditional Scottish ballad, is said to be the most widely collected song in English. Recording: *Joan Baez: How Sweet the Sound,* Razor & Tie, 2009. Performed by Joan Baez.

> *Art is news that stays news.*
> — Paraphrased from Ezra Pound, 1885–1972, American poet

PIECE 1.10. Antonín Dvořák, cello concerto in B Minor, op. 104, second movement (Adagio ma non troppo), 1894. Recording: *Dvořák: Cello Concerto; Silent Woods; Rondo (Remastered),* Sony, 1985. Performed by cellist Yo-Yo Ma and the Berliner Philharmoniker, conducted by Loren Maazel.

Piece 1.10 is especially illustrative because it opens and closes with a poignant sense of primary grief, and several such periods take place between as well, but also it is punctuated by periods of quite different (defensive) affect — anguish being the most prominent (see Chapter IV). Anguish and anger are among the most common defenses to hide or obscure the experience of natural grief. Here are three expressions of anguish (woe), wherein anger participates to a variable degree. They illustrate how the form of such defensive expression is epoch dependent. Can you date them?

1. Lacrimarum valle.
2. For ever the latter end of joy is woe,
   God knows that worldly joy is soon ago.
3. Life's a bitch, and then you die![4]

PIECE 1.11. William Shakespeare, "Sonnet 30," first published in 1609.

> When to the sessions of sweet silent thought
> I summon up remembrance of things past,
> I sigh the lack of many a thing I sought,
> And with old woes new wail my dear time's waste;
> Then can I drown an eye (unus'd to flow)
> For precious friends hid in death's dateless night,
> And weep afresh love's long since cancell'd woe,
> And moan the expense of many a vanish'd sight;
> Then can I grieve at grievances foregone,
>   And heavily from woe to woe tell o'er
>   The sad account of fore-bemoaned moan,
> Which I new pay as if not paid before:
>   But if the while I think on thee, dear friend,
>   All losses are restor'd, and sorrows end.

PIECE 1.12. Stephen Foster, "Jeanie with the Light Brown Hair," 1854. Recording: *Little Music Lovers: Lullabies*, Decca, 2009.

Performed by mezzo soprano Marilyn Horne and harpist Osian Ellis.

PIECE 1.13. Phillis Wheatley, "An Hymn to the Morning," first published 1773.[5]

> Attend my lays, ye ever honour'd nine,
> Assist my labours, and my strains refine;
> In smoothest numbers pour the notes along,
> For bright Aurora now demands my song.
>
> Aurora hail, and all the thousand dies,
> Which deck thy progress through the vaulted skies:
> The morn awakes, and wide extends her rays,
> On ev'ry leaf the gentle zephyr plays;
> Harmonious lays the feather'd race resume,
> Dart the bright eye, and shake the painted plume.
>
> Ye shady groves, your verdant gloom display
> To shield your poet from the burning day:
> Calliope awake the sacred lyre,
> While thy fair sisters fan the pleasing fire:
> The bow'rs, the gales, the variegated skies
> In all their pleasures in my bosom rise.
>
> See in the east th' illustrious king of day!
> His rising radiance drives the shadows away —
> But Oh! I feel his fervid beams too strong,
> And scarce begun, concludes th' abortive song.

How many of us think to grieve the passage of the most arresting aspect of morning as it becomes eclipsed by brighter day? And yet the feeling, I'm willing to bet, is common. Phillis Wheatley takes on the matter here in verse — to my mind to great effect. And her personal story is arresting, too: it's explored magnificently by Henry Gates, Jr.[6]

PIECE 1.14. Titian, *L'Addolorata a Mani Aperte*, 1555, Prado Museum, Madrid, Spain, oil on marble, 68 x 53 cm. Photo courtesy of Wikimedia Commons.

In Piece 1.14, the title for the painting, *L'Addolorata*, means "the grieving woman," but the term, perhaps bestowed by Titian himself, may or may not correspond to the definition we give to primary grief in this book. What do you think? Does the painting evoke natural grief (as we define it) or anguish? Remember, a work of art may evoke one feeling within the viewer while it depicts another. Piece 1.11 is a good example, and so is the book-length poem *Gabriel* by Edward Hirsch. In Piece 1.11, clearly Shakespeare describes (depicts) anguish in the first twelve lines, not grief as it's defined here; yet natural grief is evoked, via the final couplet, via our empathy (resisting identification with anguish), and via the enigmatic embedded everywhere within.

PIECE 1.15. Taj Mahal, Agra, India. Commissioned by Emperor Shah Jahan in 1632, completed 1653. Lead architect Ustad Ahmad Lahauri. Photograph (identified via Wikimedia Commons) by permission of the photographer, Yann Forget (© Yann Forget /CC-BY-SA-4.0).

PIECE 1.16. Ezra Pound, "In a Station at the Metro," first published in 1913.

> **The apparition of these faces in the crowd;**
> **Petals on a wet, black bough.**

Notice the seeming effortlessness with which the enigmatic is evoked in pieces 1.16 and 1.17, and quite the opposite for piece 1.15. Piece 1.15 evokes, for me at least, first awe, then grief. (See the commentary on awe later in this chapter.)

PIECE 1.17. Ellsworth Kelly (1923-2015). *Green Blue,* 1968. Painted aluminum, 103½ x 112½ x 68½ inches (262.9 x 285.8 x 174 cm). The Museum of Modern Art, New York. © Ellsworth Kelly Foundation.

This work evokes for me the enigmatic sublime fusion of ecstasy and sadness. Art universally arouses a sense of the enigmatic, across time and culture. Innate grief and sublimity each bear the stamp of enigma and are shadows of each other. Enigma or problem—each a surprise, a punctuation, within the stream of experience. *Enigma* prompts contemplation: thereby it is deepened (example: health).[7] *Problem* asks for solution: thereby, if one is found, it vanishes (example: illness).

PIECE 1.18. Emily Dickinson, "XXIII (Second Series)," first published 1891.

> Ample make this bed.
>   Make this bed with awe;
> In it wait till judgment break
> Excellent and fair.
>
> Be its mattress straight,
> Be its pillow round;
> Let no sunrise's yellow noise
> Interrupt this ground.

The poet's conscious intention here is awe, not sublime sadness (see below), expressed through the religious enormity of the word "judgment." For me, though, what is evoked is sublime sadness, and I am not alone. I first heard this poem, as I suspect is true for many, at the conclusion of the movie *Sophie's Choice*, a work —

true to William Styron's novel of the same title — centered with relentless intensity on uncovering essential grief.

PIECE 1.19. Paul Rotterdam, Substance 287, 1977, private collection. Acrylic on sculpted canvas, 179.7 x 121.9 cm. Personal photograph.

PIECE 1.20. Walt Whitman, "Song of Myself" (final ten lines), first published, untitled, in *Leaves of Grass*, 1855.

> I depart as air, I shake my white locks at the runaway sun,
> I effuse my flesh in eddies, and drift it in lacy jags.
>
> I bequeath myself to the dirt to grow from the grass I love,
> If you want me again look for me under your boot-soles.
>
> You will hardly know who I am or what I mean,
> But I shall be good health to you nevertheless,
> And filter and fiber your blood.
>
> Failing to fetch me at first keep encouraged,
> Missing me one place search another,
> I stop somewhere waiting for you.

PIECE 1.21. Ma Yuan, *On a Mountain Path in Spring* (detail), 1190–1225, National Gallery, Taipei, Taiwan, ink on silk, 27.4 cm × 43.1 cm.

PIECE 1.22. Phidias, *Athenia Lemnia*. Palagi head, a good Roman copy in marble (full-body original was in bronze, ca. 451–448 BCE, set on the Acropolis of Athens, Greece; later lost or destroyed).[8] The Greek goddess Athena was the dedicatee for the Acropolis and its Parthenon (Temple of Athena). Photo courtesy of Pinterest.

PIECE 1.23. Ludwig van Beethoven, symphony no. 9 in D Minor, third movement (Adagio molto e cantabile), first performed 1824. Recording: *Beethoven Symphonie no. 9*, Deutsche Grammophon, 1984. Performed by the Berliner Philharmoniker, conducted by Herbert von Karajan.

PIECE 1.24. "Shenandoah," American/Canadian folk tune from the early nineteenth century. Recording: *Songs of Comfort and Hope*, Sony Classical, 2020. Performed by pianist Kathryn Stott and cellist Yo-Yo Ma.

And where does natural grief lead, if it does?[9]

$$\left.\begin{array}{l}\text{acceptance}\\ \text{(dawning) hope}^{10}\end{array}\right\} \text{depending on circumstance}$$

What is *dawning hope*? Effortless and enigmatic — quiet optimism, either targeting a topic of the mind or diffused (a posture of the mind). A contrast to daunting hope, which is effortful, a form of exhortation for someone or oneself to accomplish something — hope with expectation to do one's best. Daunting hope is adaptive in some settings, of course, but easily weaponized by the mind as a defense against primary grief or disappointment.

What is *acceptance*? Effortless disappearances and reappearances of pleasurable images or thoughts of whom or what has been lost.

PIECE 1.25. "Amazing Grace," lyrics by John Newton (first published in 1779), set to the melody of "New Britain" by William Walker in 1835 — the most common melody for the lyrics thereafter. Recording: *Jessye Norman: Sacred Songs*, Decca, 1981. Performed by soprano Jessye Norman, the Ambrosian Singers and the Royal Philharmonic Orchestra, conducted by Alexander Gibson.

PIECE 1.26. John Keats, "To Autumn," first published in 1819.

> Season of mists and mellow fruitfulness,
>   Close bosom-friend of the maturing sun;
> Conspiring with him how to load and bless
>   With fruit the vines that round the thatch-eves run;
> To bend with apples the moss'd cottage-trees,
>   And fill all fruit with ripeness to the core;
>   To swell the gourd, and plump the hazel shells
>   With a sweet kernel; to set budding more,
> And still more, later flowers for the bees,
> Until they think warm days will never cease,
>   For Summer has o'er-brimm'd their clammy cells.
>
> Who hath not seen thee oft amid thy store?
>   Sometimes whoever seeks abroad may find
> Thee sitting careless on a granary floor,
>   Thy hair soft-lifted by the winnowing wind;
> Or on a half-reap'd furrow sound asleep,
>   Drows'd with the fume of poppies, while thy hook
>   Spares the next swath and all its twined flowers:
> And sometimes like a gleaner thou dost keep
>   Steady thy laden head across a brook;
>   Or by a cyder-press, with patient look,
>   Thou watchest the last oozings hours by hours.
> Where are the songs of Spring? Ay, where are they?

> Think not of them, thou hast thy music too, —
> While barred clouds bloom the soft-dying day,
>   And touch the stubble-plains with rosy hue;
> Then in a wailful choir the small gnats mourn
>   Among the river sallows, borne aloft
>   Or sinking as the light wind lives or dies;
> And full-grown lambs loud bleat from hilly bourn;
>   Hedge-crickets sing; and now with treble soft
>   The red-breast whistles from a garden-croft;
>   And gathering swallows twitter in the skies.

PIECE 1.27. Miles Davis, "Blue in Green." Recording: *Kind of Blue (Legacy Edition)*, Columbia, 1959. Performed by trumpeter Miles Davis, saxophonist John Coltrane, pianist Bill Evans, double bassist Paul Chambers, and drummer Jimmy Cobb.

> Davis announces his intention, via the title, to evoke sadness, and he succeeds. Of course, no such announcement was really needed — one has only to listen — and the announcement does not mean the artist will succeed. In some musical works, those making use of the blues in particular, the music evokes its announced intention and its accomplishment of it, i.e., it announces, depicts, and evokes primary grief — all wordlessly.

PIECE 1.28. Maurice Ravel, piano concerto in G Major, M. 83, second movement (Adagio assai), first performed in 1932. Recording: *Ravel Concerto en Sol, La Valse, Ma Mère L'Oye, Rapsodie Espagnole, Daphnis Et Chloé*, Warner Classics, 2012.

ART AND THE EVOCATION OF NATURAL GRIEF   45

Performed by pianist Martha Argerich and the Orchestra della Svizzera Italiana, conducted by Jacek Kaspszyk.

PIECE 1.29. Franz Schubert, "Ständchen" from *Schwanengesang*, D. 957, composed in 1828. Recording: Schubert: *Leider*, Deutsche Grammophon, 2003. Performed by baritone Dietrich Fischer-Dieskau and pianist Gerald Moore.

PIECE 1.30. Samuel Taylor Coleridge, "Frost at Midnight" (final ten lines), first published in 1798.

> Therefore all seasons shall be sweet to thee,
> Whether the summer clothe the general earth
> With greenness, or the redbreast sit and sing
> Between the tufts of snow on the bare branch
> Of mossy apple-tree, while the night thatch
> Smokes in the sun-thaw; whether the eave-drops fall
> Heard only in the trances of the blast,
> Or if the secret ministry of frost
> Shall hang them up in silent icicles,
> Quietly shining to the quiet Moon.

PIECE 1.31. John David Earnest, "Berceuse" (mvt vii), Suite for Solo Cello. Performed by Sally Singer Tuttle, recording session 20 May 2016. (Available for streaming only on SoundCloud.)

The composer wrote this comment on 23 February 2016.
A few weeks ago, an extraordinary woman I've known since 1985, Jill G., passed away. She was a lifelong friend of my longtime friend, Harvey P., who was very close

to her. I went to Jill's funeral — a cellist played movements from the Bach Suites before the service of remembrances from friends and family and played quite beautifully. As I left the service, I thought that I would write a solo piece for cello dedicated to Harvey in memory of Jill, as a tribute both to Jill and to Harvey and to their lifelong friendship and devotion to each other. I decided on a piece that would, I believe, best represent the experience of passing — a Berceuse — a gentle lullaby of remembrance and comfort.

PIECE 1.32. Samuel Jones, "Benediction (After Lutkin's Benediction and Sevenfold Amen)," 2006. Recording: *Echoes: Classic Works Transformed*, Naxos, 2011. Performed by the Seattle Symphony, conducted by Gerard Schwarz.

A nine-minute recording, moving inexorably to the fullness of sublime sadness.

PIECE 1.33. Franz Schubert, String Quintet in C Major, second movement (Adagio), composed in 1828. Recording: *Schubert: Streichquintett C-Dur*, Deutsche Grammophon, 1992. Performed by cellist Mstislav Rostropovich and the Emerson String Quartet.

An Aside on the Human Voice in Music and Its Categories

Here in Chapter I, with the exception of Piece 1.2, wherever the human voice has a role in the musical pieces that I've selected — and many of them are drawn from the classical repertoire, including opera — I emphasize its role as one instrument or more among those making the music, rather than its use in a literal sense, that of making words important to the composer's communication of sublime sadness. We realize at least three advantages from choosing such an emphasis.

First is that vocal and nonvocal pieces can be thought of interchangeably as vehicles for transmitting the composer's experience of her creation. Second is that in the process of selecting examples of music evoking sublime sadness, we are not easily misled: a composer's conception of mourning may differ considerably from, or encompass more than, our conception of natural grief; if the voice is valued musically, rather than literally, for the words it sings, a piece that advertises itself — from its title and lyrics — to be about sadness, but evokes instead a defensive feeling, like anguish, does not get into our mix of selections. Why? Because we did not in the first place make a judgment about a piece's power to evoke sublime sadness based on its title or lyrics. Third is that we have a ready explanation for a common observation: many listeners appreciate vocal musical pieces in a foreign language, one they do not understand (almost always such a piece is a classical one — an opera, for example) as much as, or even more than, they appreciate a similar piece in their own language.

Still, compositions abound in vocal music wherein the title, lyrics, or both accurately depict the sublime sadness that is musically evoked. The lyrics to Handel's Messiah are just one example from the classical repertoire. In operatic music, whenever the librettist is so brilliant as to evoke within the composer the exact feeling that he hopes the composer's music will evoke, the result, when the composer shares a comparable genius, is likely to be a perfectly corresponding music and text. Many of the operas of Mozart and of Verdi are role models.

In jazz, much of its originating energy, purpose, and style arose from the blues and from ragtime, and these genres had taken their birth from the impulse to reshape and enlarge the vocal music that Black persons subjected to slavery and their immediate descendants had created to help them bear its sadness and, later, Jim Crow — the many social injustices motivated by racism. Hence a correspondence between music and text in jazz for transmitting grief is hardly rare. At the opposite pole, so to speak, the popularization of scat singing by the trumpeter Louis Armstrong in 1927[11] and its elaboration by other jazz musicians as time passed, marks the innovative, spontaneous use of the voice musically, yet deliberately and undeniably sans any literal significance whatever.

Folk music I will define here as a music passed from generation to generation, often, not always, having been created by persons unknown, and of a plain enough musical structure that it is learned (or learnable) by ear rather than by studying a written score. Its genius, in my opinion, which it must possess to have survived, resides within its key-like property of opening the door to national or cultural identity, a feeling of belonging. If loss and therefore grief are advertised through its title or text, sublime sadness is likely evoked by its music. Time itself has picked it out for that reason and for that consequence. Some examples are presented above.

Popular music, including pop, rock, folk-pop, country, rap, hip-hop, and several other genres, is a term I will use to point to music, usually produced for a mass audience, that becomes locked within the time of its creation — imprisoned within an epoch, one relatively brief. The emotional "purpose" for its composition, whether expressive, erotic, kinetic, enlivening, or motivating, varies widely depending on genre, but the ambition, intuition, or impulse to create art that evokes the calm of sublime sadness is probably least common. Yet some popular music will do just that, evoke sublime sadness, as if innate grief, given a chance, will sneak past any intimidation by category. When and if that happens, some of these pieces will burst out of their epoch: they can no longer be restrained; they are now folk music. Something similar may take place by an alternative route. The text that is vocalized and the artistry of the vocalist may transform a song into poetry; by this extramusical dimension, it becomes sublime. See our comments on Bob Dylan's "Don't Think Twice, It's Alright" above and in Chapter IV.

From my coauthor Susan Pickett I learn that during the early Renaissance, some melodies stood, as it were, in limbo between popular and folk, so-called saloon songs. And some of these were stolen from their first venue by composers who then reworked them for choral use within the Christian mass, i.e., they were provided a new, for them, structural complexity, one typical of the most ambitious (meaning artistically ambitious) pieces of the day. They are now classical.

By classical music, I mean music of enough structural complexity to endure across generations, and that is evocative across cultures when transcultural exposure provides it the opportunity.[12] Among the aesthetic[13] experiences it is empowered to evoke, sublime sadness is most certainly a principal among them.

A Note on Sentimentality

Sentimentality is often explicitly or implicitly considered a display of inauthentic feeling, a form of dishonesty. Although I understand the impulse to so label it in some circumstances, I think, at the same time, that to purport the value and rightness of such a label in anything like a general sense is so inept as to be laughable. I once purchased formal evening wear for my mother, then in her late eighties and a widow, when she agreed to be my companion to the opera. We had a great time together, and when she died a few years after, I kept those clothes in my own closet for sentimental reasons. Each time I saw them, I smiled, thinking of her and how pleased she had been to receive them. My motive, I think, may properly be considered sentimental, but to therefore conclude that it is dishonest or inauthentic seems to me (and I'm guessing the same will be true for many of my readers) ludicrously puritanical. The complexities of the term sentimentality are well laid out in a series of three essays printed back-to-back in the Neill and Ridley volume *Arguing About Art*.[14] For the perversion that sentimentalizing may cause within the quality and worth of our thinking, feeling, and deciding about war and wartime, Elizabeth Samet provides a powerful case.[15] And an everyday exercise in sentimentality, so widespread in American culture as to exist within it as a common custom, yet one that blemishes the authenticity of its perpetrator and the self-esteem of its recipient, is now bestowed with a just title: toxic positivity.[16]

For our purposes, it will be enough to think of sentimentalizing as astonishingly pluripotential: sometimes a variant of idealization — a defense for hiding an adaptive but perhaps feared affect, such as grief, or a defense for eliding a phobic self-image, such as seeing oneself as impotent, fragmented, wicked, or invisible; sometimes a mental action serving as a place setter for an adaptive affect or experience, such as natural grief or acceptance;[17] sometimes conscious and purposeful for swaying an audience, a goal that may have a laudable motive, such as aesthetic fulfillment, education, or practical relief for those who suffer; or the opposite — a goad for unjustified, unreasoned, often prejudicial, violence.

In short, context is all — as is the frequency of sentimentalizing: from deployment quite occasional to one so unrelenting as to constitute the style of a personality. For details, see the works of Shakespeare. The full reach of the sentimental in human affairs may appear inexhaustible, including into locations wherein its worthiness is undecidable, but even so, it has its contraries: natural grief, joy, wonder, love, lust, curiosity, surprise, pride (not vanity), fear, anger (its adaptive version), and (perhaps only in context) disgust.

A Commentary on *Awe* by Comparison with *Sublime*

The meanings of words, and therefore the ways in which we put them to use, vary over time, something that's commonly understood and accepted. Even when a word's meaning is constant — as a given name, for example — the frequency with which it comes into everyday utterance and application may differ mightily from epoch to epoch, from one generation to another. On occasion we ourselves may choose just how to use a word when we might have chosen otherwise, when rivals to our choice not only exist but are vigorously employed. Our choice then is, in effect, a weighing in with an opinion about that word's best application, "best" currently at least. Such is the case with my use of the words sublime and awe.

I'll be blunt. I want these words, when I'm their speaker, to bear a relation to their origins that, to me, seems truest. There's a second thing: I want to make use of these words in a way that bears directly on their use in common, current American speech. *Sublime* was imported into English in the sixteenth century from the Latin *sublimis/sublime*, possibly from French as well, and its meaning was this: raised up, high, lofty, tall — applicable to a building, a column, the cost of mutton, or to a style or accomplishment. In English, from the beginning, its application was considered poetic, even when applied literally to a height. By the eighteenth century, it began to take on a sense of flight, soaring flight in particular. An example from the *Oxford English Dictionary* (OED): "the sublime flight of a poet."

And by the end of that century, its application to a supreme aesthetic feeling had matured enough for overt commentary. My reasons for concluding that an experience of the sublime bears an embodiment of natural grief, and has for millennia, are presented at length in the Introduction and in Chapter VI. I am aware that philosophers and scholars, from Immanuel Kant onward, often insist that sublime may describe rapture, yes, within an aesthetic response to art or nature (Kant seems to have had nature, solely, in mind), but also may be used synonymously with awe.[18] I object. Few beyond their circle talk (or write) that way anymore; the rest of us reserve sublime for the most positive degree of aesthetic[19] experience, regardless of its source — art, nature, or social.

Awe, according to the OED, was imported from Scandinavia into English in the twelfth century with a meaning of fear, dread, or terror. As time passed, the word became especially indicative of one's self-concern in relation to the power of God; from there, fear of and reverence for God; and from there, reverence for a person of great authority or accomplishment. By the eighteenth century, awe is used to express wonder or fear inspired by the power or beauty within the natural world.

I think that *sublime* and *awe* are each a word, along with a third word, *wonder*, for an experience wherein enigma is the essential and shared ingredient, that enigma is their holding in common, creating of them an enigma-based triad. Each affect holds its place individually: *sublime* is the enigmatic, calm fusion of sadness and ecstasy triggered by loss, loss that's real or imagined; *awe* is the experience of being small in the presence of vastness, an enigmatic, energized fusion of ecstasy and fear; *wonder* is the enigmatic pleasure of surprise fused with curiosity, whether what one is surprised by, yet intensely curious about, lies within oneself or without — it energizes perhaps midway between the sublime and awe.

This formulation of individual members of a triad governs my use of these three words for this book. Within any given aesthetic experience, one may dominate — and perhaps this is most common — or may exist interfused sequentially or back and forth with one or both of the others, depending on the evocative stimulus within the occasion, on the state-of-mind of the observer, or both. For me, as I've said, and I'd suppose for many, our piece 1.15, a photo of the Taj Mahal, first evokes awe, owing to its size and the force of its symmetries. But as I sit with it, especially when I welcome within my memory that it too is a memory, one of a much beloved spouse, a spouse entombed within it, then sublime sadness replaces my awe.

It is just such potential interfusion, I'd guess, that has prompted Dacher Keltner and his several colleagues and collaborators to agree with one another that all three affects within my triad may be subsumed under just one name, awe — discussed in considerable detail in Keltner's recent book, *Awe*. Much as I am awed, however, by the persistence and magnitude of Keltner's pursuit of this subject, I cannot agree. I feel little awe or wonder when I sit with a grieving person's achingly calm, ravishingly beautiful sadness.

Nor can I agree with Keltner's position about the "size" of the observing self during an experience of awe, wonder, or the sublime. He employs over and over terms like "the vanishing of the self" in such a circumstance. But this can't, in my estimation, be true. Am I ever more alive, and sizeable, than I am just then? Better might be to say that who I am is "translocated" while I'm under the spell of one of the enigma-based affects, translocated from a place wherein I'm alert to taking action to a place wherein I'm wholly an observer, albeit one bearing intense feeling. And what I'm observing is placed externally to me on the one hand but includes me and my state of feeling on the other. It's not that I am less egocentric; it's that my ego is spellbound, and I know it. (Part of Keltner's viewpoint flows from studies he cites suggesting experiences of the enigma-based affects for a time make us more generous toward others, but I fail to see why we should presume we are less egocentric when we are more generous — to think so would imply that the "me" and the "other" in a perceptual circumstance make up a zero-sum game, i.e., that more of one implies less of the other).

NOTES

1. I hold to the notion that an artwork, including music, evokes aesthetic feeling in its beholder that originated (whether consciously or not) within the mind of the artist who authored the work and has been interpreted by the artists who perform it (where performers are needed for the work's actualization). A parallel to my belief is that an artwork itself, such as a piece of music, has not by itself, somehow freed from its creators, become expressive of aesthetic feeling. For a view opposed to mine, see the preprint for an article in, or about to be in, *The Journal of Aesthetic Education* entitled "On the Value of Sad Music" by Mario Attie-Picker, Tara Venkatesan, George E. Newman, and Joshua Knobe; a link to the preprint is provided by Oliver Whang in his article for The New York Times of May 19, 2023 ("Why Do We Listen to Sad Songs?"). See also, Saam Trivedi, "Resemblance Theories."
2. See Droitcour, "The View from Inside" in *Art in America*, 26–27.
3. Mentioned by Scruton, *Beauty*, 115.
4. All three expressions claim that life is *mainly* about loss; the third one does so tongue-in-cheek. The first is the Latin expression for "valley of tears" and is taken from the prayer *Salve Regina*, composed in the eleventh century or earlier — a lament on the tribulation of mortal life at a time when median life-span was about 30 years. Death of someone you knew was part of the everyday. The second is taken from Geoffrey Chaucer's *Canterbury Tales* ("The Nun's Priest's Tale"), written in 1393. Median lifespan had not changed from 300 years earlier or, indeed, from that of Greek and Roman antiquity. The third appears first in print in October 1982 in the Washington Post, quoting fifteen-year-old Tony Daniels (see *https://quoteinvestigator.com/2016/10/16/life-hard/*). In the 1990s it became a line in a rap song. Why can it be tongue-in-cheek? Because by 1982, median life-span is 75 years.
5. See, for example, Wheatley, "Poems on Various Subjects, Religious and Moral," *Complete Writings*.
6. See Gates, *The Trials of Phillis Wheatley*.

7. See Gadamer, *Enigma of Health*.
8. See Grant, *Classical Greeks*, 78–79.
9. Prompted by John Bowlby's discussion of loneliness among the bereaved, widows in particular (Bowlby, *Loss*, 102–3), I conclude that a persistent experience of natural grief, entirely consistent with a coexisting experience of emotional loneliness, may lie within the expected state of full resolution of loss if good fortune declines to bring another attachment figure — a person with whom mutual commitment takes hold, one to replace the one lost — into their affections, i.e., natural grief need not remit for mourning to be complete. Nor does such an intrapsychic evolution at all preclude a coexisting state of acceptance, as I've defined it above, from having taken hold as well. On the other hand, if good fortune does bring a new attachment figure, such as a committed lover, natural grief in relation to the formerly bereaved figure may indeed remit and be replaced wholly by acceptance.
10. A note about hopelessness. Hopelessness cannot exist on the domain of natural grief/(dawning) hope/acceptance; there's no room for it. Hopelessness is the absence of both (dawning) hope and innate grief. It is maladaptive, by definition, the result of a violent (unconsciously executed) self-assault, just as Dante suggests in the famous ninth line of verse posted, he imagines, above the gateway to Hell: "Lasciate ogni speranza, voi ch'entrate" ("Dash all hope, ye who enter here") (*L'Inferno*, canto 3, my translation; for the line in Italian, see Alighieri, *La Divina Commedia*, Vol. I: Inferno, 22).
11. Encyclopaedia Britannica, s.v. "scat," accessed November 23, 2021, *https://www.britannica.com/art/scat-music*.
12. See Gopnik, "Human Potential."
13. In this book, our use of the word "aesthetic" will comply for the most part with the defining features described by de Bolla (*Art Matters*), with two exceptions. See 19, below.
14. See Savile, "Sentimentality," 337–41; Newman, "Alleged Unwholesomeness," 342–53; and Pugmire, "Sentimentality and Truthfulness," 354–59.
15. Samet, *Good War*, esp. 320–31.
16. See Goodman, *Toxic Positivity*.
17. When what I have called here a *mental action* is transferred (unconsciously) to an object, that object may serve a useful (i.e., adaptive) purpose as a *transitional object of grief*. Such an object may be thought

of as representing the lost person, if the mourned loss is that of a person, in the same way that the transitional object of childhood (the blankie or rag doll, for example, carried everywhere by the child) represents the secure personhood of the mother that the child both wants some independence from and yet fears being absent from at the same time — a concept, as is well known, famously identified and described by the British psychoanalyst and pediatrician Donald Winnicott. See Goldstein et al, "Transitional Objects of Grief," a phrase that fits well with my choosing to preserve my mother's clothes for the opera within my own closet after her death. Such an object is usually a calming influence for the person in mourning, but not for every such person (again, see Goldstein et al.).

18. See, for example, Esanu, *Mimesis, Expression, Construction*, esp. Lecture Three.
19. In this book, the use of "aesthetic" will correspond to the sense developed by de Bolla (*Art Matters*, see his Introduction and Chapter 5, especially) with two exceptions: we do not restrict the term, as he does, to artistic applications solely; we do not agree that the term refers to a version of an affect unique, and exclusively so, to each "object" that occasions it — we consider it to possess not only an affective component unique to its different settings but also a component general to all such settings as well, Kant's insistence on a strictly subjective origin notwithstanding.

CHAPTER II

Evocation of Sublime Sadness: Jazz and Popular Music

Mark G. Brown

I HAVE CHOSEN here a number of pieces, jazz or popular, all of which have been provided at least one iconic performance within the last forty years and most of which were created during this time. They are to illustrate the identity inherent in the juxtaposition of experiencing sublimity on the one hand and grief on the other. A compendium of popular music through all the ages cannot exist, owing to the nature of popular music, thus the number of pieces that might have served my purpose I cannot know. I must go with what I do know, which are those pieces within my lifetime as a listener and a musician that float into my awareness as I think about the feeling, sublime sadness, described in the Introduction and illustrated in Chapter I.

I am a songwriter. I choose songs, therefore, hardly a surprise, for my present purpose. Here's my description of a song:

music, relatively brief, yet complete in itself, in which lyrics are vital — not only for their musical quality but also as words whose meaning contributes to and corresponds to the complete musical and emotional intention of the piece. The one exception to song among my selections is an instrumental jazz piece that I love too much to omit.

I believe that music has the capacity to serve as a symbol — as described by the theologian Paul Tillich:[1] it points to a reality underneath the current reality wherein the receiver is invited to participate. In other words, music can prompt the listener to a deeper feeling than that provoked through its auditory property alone, hence the experience of sublime sadness — grief.

Just for example, and a very personal one: When my mother died, nearly twenty-five years ago, I discovered Henryk Górecki's Symphony No. 3. I found myself listening to it repeatedly, moved by the almost imperceptible beginning strains in the lowest register, the gradual development of volume within the strings as the theme builds, and then its gradual descent into the original, introductory notes. This piece, with its perfect symmetry and its intentional and successful evocation of grief, for me was transformative: I could begin to heal from the loss. It had provided a Tillichean symbol: I was prompted to a dimension beyond my usual range of experience from the sounds of music in themselves.

Here, now, are some pieces from popular music and from jazz bearing that same evocative power.[2] Hyperlinks to the recordings I am suggesting here are provided by this book's website (*www.thesublimesadness.com*), but choose another recording if you wish, based on the streaming service(s) most easily and customarily available to you.

PIECE 2.1. Jackson Browne, "For a Dancer." Recording: *The Very Best of Jackson Browne* (2014 Remaster), Rhino/Elektra, 2014. Produced by Al Schmidt and Jackson Browne for Asylum Records, 1974. Performed by Jackson Browne. Written by Browne in his late twenties after a close friend had died, this song expresses the experience of grief at a relatively young age:

> *I don't know what happens when people die*
> *Can't seem to grasp it as hard as I try*
> *It's like a song that I hear playing right in my ear*
> *That I can't sing, but I can't help listening*

The lyrics go on to unfold a progression: learning from the models of grieving you see before you in others, the inevitable solitude of mortality, and finally, confronting the possible futility of having lived at all. Note especially David Lindley's haunting violin solo at the end, daring to finish on the third scale note rather than the tonic, as if to suggest the experience of grief at this young age is only tentatively felt, yet ongoing.

PIECE 2.2. Frances Landesman and Thomas J. Wolf Jr., "Ballad of the Sad Young Men." Recording: *Roberta Flack: First Take*, Atlantic Records, 1968, reissued 1995. Performed by Roberta Flack.

The lyrics speak of loneliness, superficial joviality, and the emptiness of the unnatural light embedded within a city's nightlife. They go on to dark developments that touch young lives, presentiment of mortality, and the relentless decline brought on by aging. The spare instrumental treatment reinforces the theme of loneliness, particularly the string bass in its solitary, solid presence grounding the whole piece. The lyrics, in short, set the context for the experience that this voice and its accompaniment evoke musically: sublime sadness.

All the sad young men, singing in the cold
Trying to forget that that they're growing old
All the sad young men, choking on their youth
Trying to be brave, running from the truth

PIECE 2.3. Judy Collins, "Secret Gardens." Recording: *On a Winter's Night: Winter Love Songs*, Rounder Records, 2004. Produced by Christine Lavin. Performed by Judy Collins.

Collins sings of figures and scenes within a childhood from the perspective of a return to its location many years later. In her "secret gardens of the heart," the old stay young forever, untouched by the ravages and vicissitudes of time. She has juxtaposed the changes wrought by time with the permanence of preserved memory. The conflict of the remembered past and the present reality could hardly be more defiant: neither side can, nor should, yield. In this way, the singer-writer insistently resists, in my view, defensive triumph. Loss is loss, poignant because true. Accepting it as such permits her experience, so ours too, of sublime peace.

I've written a song designed to match this same plain reckoning, with these lyrics:

So strange to see our world slowly disappear
Like a fading set of footprints
Like a song I cease to hear
I see them fade away, the sacred and profane
As they bow to one last curtain
As they break one final plane

PIECE 2.4. Bob Dylan, "It's Not Dark Yet." Recording: *Wonder Boys: Music from the Motion Picture*, Columbia/Sony Music Soundtrax, 2000. Produced by Daniel Lanois. Performed by Bob Dylan.

This song from the later part of Dylan's long career evokes grief anticipatory of advancing age and decline — entropy inherent within existence and inevitable death. Here is despair over aging ("Time is running away" and "I can't even hear the murmur of a prayer"), yes, yet interwoven with a sublime sadness — the portal to acceptance beyond resignation.

PIECE 2.5. "Sometimes I Feel Like a Motherless Child," Black American folk song (spiritual); an early public performance dates to the 1870s (Fisk Jubilee Singers); the score was first written down in 1899 (William E. Barton). Recording: *Odetta*, Discos Cada, 2011. Performed by Odetta.

I heard a version of this song when my mother died, a circumstance that prompted an understanding of the impetus for its creation in a new way, new for me. There is no loneliness more powerfully contained — symbolically and actually — than that within the image of the motherless child, something you will not know until you experience the death of your own mother. I have chosen Odetta's recording because of the haunting sound in her voice and, too, a mournful quality I find to be exquisitely beautiful, combined with the musical moaning in the choral voices beneath hers. No defense against grief is called out — it goes directly to calm sadness, to the sublime experience of it, a form of surrender and from there, for me, a descent to the core of my being.

PIECE 2.6. Mark Brown, "Goodbye, Old Friend." Recording: *Words & Music*, OA2 Records, 2008. Performed by Mark Brown (vocals, blues harp, trumpet) and pianist Paul West.

One of my own songs, written on the death, at age 53, of a friend I'd known since age 14. I believe, quite obviously, that it evokes sublime sadness, or I would not include it here. It may be thought of, too, as an argument, one that goes like this: those we are close to in life, on their death, are irreplaceable there, in life, even as they become permanent within our minds (so that we may write songs about them). Seeing that gap, insisting that I do, between life on the one hand and my mind on the other, is how I honor such a person, one irreplaceable, gone, yet never absent. My horn solo at the end is, in my opinion, a figuration of authentic grief: my friend fading as the natural distance grows yet never absent.

PIECE 2.7. Joaquín Rodrigo, "Concierto de Aranjuez," written in 1939. Recording: *Concierto*, CTI Records,1975. Produced by Creed Taylor. Performed by the Jim Hall Sextet (Jim Hall, Paul Desmond, Chet Baker, Ron Carter, Steve Gadd, and Roland Hanna).

One of my favorite jazz performances ever, a version of this very often performed and recorded jazz classic (see also just one of many, many examples: Miles Davis on his *Sketches of Spain* album). Some of its glories: Ron Carter's bass; the insistent Latin rhythm; the solos by Roland Hanna (piano) and Paul Desmond (saxophone); the highlight for me, though, is Chet Baker's trumpet solo at the end, with the virtuoso, unforgettable gesture of his partially depressing a single valve — the longing evoked by a poignant sigh.

NOTES

1. Rowe, "Tillich's Theory," 593.
2. *Editorial note:* In this chapter it's best to find the recording that Brown has specified for each piece, if possible, because his comments, to be fully appreciated, depend on it. As of this writing, each is available on Amazon Music and on Spotify, whereas Apple Music, YouTube Music, and SoundCloud are missing one or more, although they have available other recordings of each (SoundCloud does not have piece 2.6).

CHAPTER III

A Work of Art and a Nation's Grief

Grief and Art Are Here Indivisible

a short fiction[1] by

ROBERT ARNOLD JOHNSON

On this day Will first knew the feeling that has so puzzled him since. Well, it's not a feeling really. Feeling means emotion. Right? Yes, it does, in common speech at least. So, we often instead say sense. And the dictionary agrees; it ranks it high among the possible senses for sense. But then the dictionary goes on to define this particular sense of sense as a feeling.

Will is a mathematician: to him, this is double-talk, and it bothers him. (Now bother, there's a feeling for you.) What is it then? This "kinda" feeling? In Will's case on that day, I'd guess it's a form of wondering: did I know or didn't I? And that special case for wondering in which I can never know the answer about my knowing. And why not? Because it's undecidable. We have a hard time with words for the undecidable. The situations they bear on have the stamp of the uncanny about them. We don't easily come up with words for the uncanny. I'm a litterateur; for me, it's easier, part of my job description, to bear such uneasiness, enjoy it even. But Will, as I've mentioned, is a mathematician. The uncanny bothers him more than it does me. And that's in his job description, to be bothered more than most of us by the uncanny. Maybe, after all, feeling for the sense I'm talking about is not so bad.

What Will told me was the sense he knew this day would come, the day when he knew for the first time for sure what he'd earlier known, all the while unaware that he knew it. True, the way and when of its coming he could lay no claim to knowing, but the fact of it. So odd. An answer he thought he wanted, one to a dreadful question. When it appeared, he felt he'd known it all along. The "all along": when did the knowledge such phrasings lay claim to really commence? Was it in the summer following his sophomore year of college, J's too? (J, just J, had been his friend's nickname since fourth grade.)

Will recalls a particular day of that summer, the one stacking hay bales when J made clear that ROTC had been for him the highlight of being in college, so far at least, and he, J, had decided he'd enlist, begin a career in the army, immediately on graduation. Will's opposition to the war in Vietnam was embryonic back then — well, maybe fetal — not mature enough to yet impose on him a distinct moral misgiving about the implication in J's short speech. No, this intuition of foreknowledge would have had to do with death, J's death. And just maybe it had been there even before, even from their first junior high days together, based on some premonition about a warrior brooding within J and the end that warrior could, or was likely to, prematurely come to.[2] Could Will's feeling that he knew J's fate have originated even so far back as that, junior high school, eight years or so preceding their discussion around the hay bales?

In sum, then, if Will had known "all along," when did that sense of knowing commence? Undecidable. And had he known, in fact, or did he only feel now, abruptly in retrospect, like he felt he had or might have? Undecidable and uncanny. When did the full force of the uncanny burst upon Will's awareness? At least this much is decidable. May 31, 1984, when he'd visited the Vietnam Veterans Memorial in Washington, DC, for the first time, twenty years to the day after he'd last seen J in person, then so alive and full to overflowing with a warrior's confidence. On May 31, 1984, he'd found J's name on the wall.

For more than two years after college graduation, Will would hear from J by letter every few weeks. He learned that J was immediately commissioned a second lieutenant, based on his college ROTC training, and he knew that within a year J had been deployed to Vietnam, then promoted in rank a year later. Soon after, abruptly: no more letters. Three or four months after the last of these, the one that time would prove to be the final one, Will attempted to call J's paternal grandparents, who had raised him. But their telephone had been disconnected. So, he sent them a letter of inquiry; it was returned. Only when more years had gone by did he learn from a high school classmate that both grandparents had died within the year following J's departure for Vietnam. The classmate had himself moved away soon after, so he knew nothing about what had come of J.

Will's own connection with Prineville, Oregon, the community of his and J's growing up, had been severed during Will's final year in college, his parents having sold their ranch to enable them to join Will's older, married sister and her family in another state. Later, he wondered, too, if he had made an excuse of that event, his parents' move, to void any reason for making a return, any return, even just one, to Prineville on his own, one designed to query those friends and acquaintances there who'd known J and may have learned something about his fate during the war. Had it been easier not to know? And still more years passed: thoughts of J came to mind with ever diminishing frequency, approaching zero yet never reaching it. At the same time, the poignancy of the thought, when it came, seemed always keener than ever before — an odd equilibrium of sorts.

Will's path had taken him from college on to grad school in math at MIT in Cambridge, Massachusetts, a path beginning immediately after he parted from J on their commencement day. Student deferments from the military draft lasted just until he was a new PhD, the U.S. Army having already decided it must make use of him, cash in, so to speak, on its investment in his vocational skills.

Although his graduate work had incorporated much of what would be called now systems modeling, by a quirk of fate he escaped assignment to the cadre of such experts who would later share culpability for the narrowness of thinking that caused President Lyndon Johnson and Secretary of Defense Robert McNamara to misjudge the winnability of the war.[3] That quirk was this: Will had gained a reputation at MIT as an especially gifted instructor and mentor for undergraduate math students. The chairperson for mathematics at West Point, who paid attention to ongoing gossip from MIT, got wind of this and was able to persuade the Army to assign Will directly to the West Point faculty as an instructor in math. Will happily complied. He was encouraged to continue his research program there too. Once the war ended, he stayed on as a faculty civilian at West Point for a few more years, next accepting a position at a large public university in New York state.

Early in 1981, Will read that a group of Vietnam War veterans were raising money to build a memorial to the American casualties of that war in Washington, DC. It was to be placed within a plot on the National Mall, its design decided via a national competition — one indeed already under way — and it must contain the name of each of the fallen. He sent a contribution, promising himself that once the memorial was no longer a dream, a hope, but real, he'd carry through with what he'd so long postponed, settling the answer to a question — perhaps question wants the definite article the in this case — about his friend J.

He arrived, as I've mentioned, on a beautiful final day of May three years later. For one or more reasons he was unable ever to specify, he'd looked at no published photos or descriptions beforehand — a visit he was later to call virginal. At a glance, he saw the place was no memorial to war, a war in Vietnam or anywhere else. It was instead the visual equivalent of a solemn, sad psalm for the American dead of that war — not a paean to heroes but something like a choir singing verses sacred of the fallen, their names come to rest there. He took a small notebook from his pocket, realizing, rarely for him, an obligation to his thought, when it was a nonmathematical example of thought, and thereby to his feelings. A phrase, one common from his childhood, "this day of all days," was the first thing he wrote. The second thing was the word I've reported already, "psalm."

The form embodying the psalm was a carved, clean V into the earth. On the one hand, a gouge, a gash, on the other, an incision, one made by an artist bearing a surgeon's intentionality.[4] The arms of the V seemed of equal length, extending from the vertical line of their union — the V's vertex — outward as an embrace, a welcoming, and at the same time a lift of wings from their gentle tilt upward from the vertex. A paradox then: the vigor borne from a violent creation; yet once the creation's complete, a peace. Mother Earth, a birthing from her, yet now a landscape, accepting itself bearing the loss it's made from. Will wrote a comment about the grass, the lawn running to the topside margin of the V and up relatively close to its downside margin, that it accentuates the sense of human-made incision he'd noted first yet simultaneously promotes the principle of unintimidated botanical fertility. Still another paradox.

A duality flows from the form within which this psalm is written: the names it enshrines, easily glimpsed from a distance, may be compared with two sides of a coin grasped in one vision: buried below ground within their sepulcher and yet exposed to their freestanding public of onlookers, the curious, the awed, the grieving. Death and life mated, matched. As he came closer, ever more stunned by the sheer number of those named, this thought came to mind, which he stopped to write out: "Most of us visiting are looking for one name in particular, I'll bet; to one name we are preparing our full attention among so many, many; yet this magnificent place, an artwork of place, will not permit us to ignore for long its great sum — an ingenious twist or wrinkle on the usual reading of 'E pluribus unum.'"

He must have looked the part of someone having shown up "virginally," to make use of his own sense of himself there, as he was soon noticed by an attendant, who explained how to find any single name on the wall — a phrase meant to include the two V arms as one — a name that might be of special importance to him, and also some facts about the order and number of names: their presentation according to date of casualty; the meeting of the names — those of the first casualties and those of the last — together at the V's vertex in the center. The attendant also pointed out, both pointed literally and in the sense of "pointing out," with a smile, that the V's east arm directs one's gaze to the Washington Monument in the distance and the west arm directs the gaze to the Lincoln Memorial.

Each arm of the wall is composed of 70 black granite panels that are highly polished, and it is on these panels, of course, into which the names have been engraved and on which the sky, its clouds (or not), the purlieu surrounding, and the visitors, most in rapt attendance, are mirrored. Death and life: with one, the other; minus one, minus the other; here they're woven together.

Will put away pen and notebook, found J's name at the nearest ledger podium and then its engraving on the wall, there on a panel for those fallen in 1966. J's death had come, his life had extended, just thirty months after he and Will held their last face-to-face chat, an interval corresponding with the duration of letters. He'd learned that day that J had written to him so long as he could — so long as he could — ever and forever. With reading J's name in this place, this psalm-like place, an unknown about J's life vanished, replaced by an undecidable something, a something foreknown within Will's mind.

"It was like a phase-shift in a state of a substance, like water into steam," was Will's comment to me, reviewing what I've written here. "I'm going to ask something really silly," he went on. "Could that explain my wet cheeks on that day? Could that place, my experience of it and within it, could that for me have prompted a phase shift of myself, to one with wet cheeks? A 'myself' transposed into a warm, moist peace, like calm steam?"

"It's your tears, trickle tears," I said. "When did you first notice them? Was it when you found J's name, either in the directory or engraved on the wall?"

"No," he answered. "It was before that. It was walking into and becoming immersed within that place."

NOTES

1. A fictional story. Would that be true for all similar stories that might be told, those based on friendship in the 1960s. Each of the photographs of the Vietnam Veterans Memorial is licensed to us by iStock.
2. See Duthie, *Return to Saigon*, 280. In this memoir about his own participation as a combatant in the Vietnam War, Duthie comments about what he calls "The Wish," an awareness that dawns at some point, or may do so, perhaps quite suddenly, within the warrior's own mind. The awareness sounds something like this: "I want to, I hope I will, live to die old of 'natural causes.'" The intuition I speak of in Will's mind is the flip side: his friend J's experience of "The Wish," the hope embedded within it, if and when it occurs to him, will go unfulfilled.
3. See Heineman, "Idolatry of Numbers."
4. Here, the artist's intentionality belongs, as is well known, to Maya Lin, who won the competition — in which contestants were judged anonymously — for the memorial's design at age 21, while she was an undergraduate at Yale, a career launch conjuring that of Leonardo, Mozart, Keats, Schubert, and Picasso.

CHAPTER IV

Musical Structure and Sublime Sadness[1]

Susan Eileen Pickett

For Raphael's *Madonna del Granduca*, (Piece 1.3), sublime sadness is depicted within the facial expression of the madonna, at least for some observers of it; the human element feels immediate to the viewer. We may see the Vietnam Veterans Memorial similarly: over fifty-eight thousand names of people etched on black granite. Songs of any genre — also Western classical music that includes text (opera or lieder) — prompt listeners to hear the music through the lens of the words. But what about absolute music, that is, music without a text or a programmatic story? How might this music depict sublime sadness?

For non-musicians, a bit of terminology will be helpful. Composers indicate the **tempo** of a piece at the very beginning of a work. Most often, Italian terms such as *allegro* (fast) or *lento* (slowly), and dozens of others, tell the performer, generally, about its pace. Here we'll think of tempo as how fast or slow the listener is inclined to tap her foot to the beat of the music. **Dynamics** tell the performer how loudly or softly to play. While the first dynamics used in music were simply forte (loudly, shown as *f*) and piano (softly, shown as *p*), over several centuries these distinctions were further graded from *ffff* (very, very, very, very loudly) to *pppp*.

Sometimes, composers overtly specify the **mood** of a work (or a section of it) by using a term, such as *doloroso* (sorrowful) or *dolce* (sweet). Also, composers may use **pitch** — its location within the range of an instrument or a voice — known as its *register*, for emotional impact. The highest registers of an instrument, including a singer's voice, tend to be more "tense" (especially if loud) than the lowest registers. In fact, for example, when a soprano sings very softly and calmly in a high register, it is usually a surprise for the listener, which brings its own emotional impact.

Melody, which means a sequence through time of musical pitches, has had a central role in Western music from its origin. The earliest examples that we have of music that was written down (as music's notation evolved) were just single melodies, without notated accompaniment.[2] And the twentieth century contains the other extreme, the (relative) demotion of melodic importance: some composers downgraded it, substituting an emphatic rhythmic innovation or augmenting the force of some one or more of other musical elements. Stravinsky's *Rite of Spring* is a prime example: a great composition that does not depend on melody (nor is it a piece that brings sublime sadness to the forefront). By now, however, we have the advantage of hindsight. We see that much of the music of the twentieth century that has for audiences survived the test of time does, in fact, contain memorable melody. The currently active American composer Samuel Jones insists that melody is an important tool for etching music in the memory of its listeners.[3] When I discuss the compositions that we have chosen to illustrate the feeling of sublime sadness, I will have more to say about the role of melody.

Momentum is the word I'll use to describe whether the listener either feels being pulled forward by the music or is, instead, inclined to luxuriate within the moment. Momentum may be thought of physically. Is the music conducive to a brisk walk? A leisurely stroll? Standing still? Sprinting? Momentum is primarily determined by tempo and rhythm.[4] It is also affected by the frequency of chord changes. Think about "America (My Country, 'Tis of Thee)" — every syllable has a different chord; thus, there's rapid harmonic rhythm, i.e., a rapid pace of harmonic change, and that provokes a sense of momentum. On the opposite end of the spectrum, "Silent Night" changes chords far less frequently, offering more repose.

Texture is a common term in music. Here I'll stick with a basic aspect of texture, that is, whether there is one primary melody by itself (a very simple texture), a primary melody with accompaniment (often a fairly simple texture), or two or more nearly equally important melodies simultaneously (a more complex texture).

Western music written within the common practice period (1600–1900) is based on what is called the *major-minor system*, that is, it's written in a major key or a minor key. It is often said that music in minor keys tends to be sadder than music in major keys, and for some performers and composers, certain minor keys are perceived as being more melancholic than others: D minor, F-sharp minor, and G-sharp/A-flat minor. But a claim that music evoking sadness implies a minor key is much too generalized, and the same is true of the claim in reverse, that a minor key ensures the evocation of sadness. I'd point out that most patriotic music is in a major key ("My Country, 'Tis of Thee"); so are many holiday tunes, and so are many hymns. Well-known music in a minor key includes the first movement of Beethoven's famous fifth symphony — a portion of which I'll discuss shortly.

Printed music tells the performers about tempo, dynamics, key, sometimes mood, and (loosely[5]) momentum. I will examine these several elements in a sample of the musical compositions we have chosen (Chapters I and II) to show how they contribute to evoking sublime sadness. But first, let's examine a composition that is not on the list: the first movement of Beethoven's fifth symphony, which, we would argue, is most definitely not conducive to sublime sadness. In fact, it is frequently characterized as stormy. Why? Its tempo is *Allegro con brio* (fast, with spirit or brilliance). It has nearly unrelenting momentum, one so beyond a brisk walk it's an all-out sprint. While it does have passages that are soft (*piano*), most of them immediately crescendo (gradually get louder), heightening momentum further still. Also, much of this movement is either *f* or *ff*. Most of it is based on the famous opening motive, the pervasiveness of which could be likened to a nail being hit by a hammer over and over: it evokes variously restlessness, storminess, anger, even torment. Yes, it's great music, but it is neither sublime nor sad.

What Is Different When Music Evokes Sublime Sadness?

Compare the movement of Beethoven's fifth symphony I've just discussed to a work that is indeed on our sublime sadness list: the third movement of **Beethoven's ninth symphony** (Piece 1.22). The initial tempo instruction is *Adagio molto e cantabile* — very slow and in a singing style. The movement begins softly and with a simple texture. In an unusual twist, Beethoven does not immediately launch into one of the main melodies. Instead, the first fifteen seconds[6] are a quiet introduction, perhaps calming the usual listener, who has just heard the raucous second movement. Then the first main melody (A) is heard in the violins. It is calm, owing to its tempo, its dynamic, its harmonic rhythm, and its texture.

Also, calm is amplified by use of a particular melodic device: most of the sequential pitches (melodic intervals) are relatively close together (seconds, thirds, fourths). Larger leaps in sequential pitch (larger intervals) would have added tension; this melody is one that's more like rolling hills than jagged peaks. Combined, these five elements, then, elicit sublime sadness. At 2:40 into the movement, Beethoven alters the tempo to *Andante moderato*, which might be thought of as the pace of a leisurely stroll. A new melody (theme B) is introduced: its register is higher, the dynamic is louder, and the texture more complex (because of countermelodies played simultaneously by some sections of the orchestra). Its structure contains mostly steps (few large intervals), so it's still overall evocative of sublime sadness; we are encouraged to stroll.

Compare what I've just said with an experience of viewing the Vietnam Veterans Memorial. When catching the first glimpse of the memorial, a person might be most inclined to stand still, draw in a breath, and just look (theme A). Then, after a few minutes, she will likely begin to stroll toward the wall, experiencing simultaneously the beauty of the memorial and the tragedy that it embodies (theme B).

In the symphony, at about 4:00, momentum changes. The conductor's tempo hasn't changed, but the listener's foot taps faster, because the string instruments pluck frequently. This section draws on theme A, heard in the first couple of minutes of the movement, but here the melody is elaborated — a variation on what we heard at the beginning. It is more complex, but it will sound familiar.

So too, at the memorial, once we have seen the wall for the first time and strolled toward it, we are prepared for more complexity, to view more of its details and to see it from different angles. We experience the variation on the movement's first melody in a similar way. At 6:00, Beethoven treats the second melody similarly: we first heard it at 2:40, and now we hear a variation, one with more complexity and momentum. Theme A then returns, with even more elaboration and thus more momentum.

Next are two brief passages that are not evocative of sublime sadness. The first, at 12:15, is a fanfare featuring brass instruments, lasting just a few seconds; the main themes then return, which may surprise the listener. Perhaps this is a parallel to the moment when the person viewing the Vietnam Veterans Memorial first encounters a name of someone they've known on the wall. The second passage at 12:40 is a similar brass fanfare, one that quietly turns darker and more somber for about fifteen seconds, at which point we then return to the sublime melodies. Beethoven has taken us on a journey. True, there are only two melodies, but they are heard with such variation that, to continue my Veterans' Memorial metaphor, we've seen the memorial from many different angles, in varying amounts of sunlight, and with ever increasing attention to detail.

The second movement of **Beethoven's violin concerto** (Piece 1.5), shares many of the features of the slow movement of his ninth symphony: a slow tempo, mostly quiet dynamics, a slow harmonic rhythm, relatively simple texture, and two melodies that are straightforward in their initial presentations and then elaborated or varied. Here, too, the melodies are made up mainly of small intervals.

Since it is a concerto, however, a solo violin line is nearly always present, and in it the composer exploits the full gamut of pitches the instrument can produce, especially those that shimmer in its highest range. At the beginning, the orchestra plays the main theme — the solo has yet to sound. When the soloist enters, the orchestra retains the main theme while the soloist, in essence, responds to the orchestra — a call-and-response structure. I'll liken this to a parallel: the orchestra represents the Vietnam Memorial and the solo violin the person reacting to it. At 4:30, the second melody appears for the first time, but it's the soloist playing it, accompanied soothingly by the orchestra, with elaborations. This melody, too, has few leaps, except one that's particularly poignant, at 5:06: breathtaking.

Unlike the ninth symphony's slow (third) movement, here in the violin concerto there are no interludes straying from the evocation of sublime sadness until its very end, when Beethoven prepares the listener for the sprightly final movement. We listeners may then move from the experience of sublimity to that of joy.

Turning now to jazz, I'll take up **"Blue in Green"** (Piece 1.26), composed by Miles Davis. Unlike the works I've discussed thus far, which have large orchestras, "Blue in Green" is for a small jazz ensemble: trumpet, saxophone, piano, string bass, and drums. There are some similarities to the works already discussed: slow tempo, soft dynamics, simple texture, slow harmonic rhythm, and the importance of melody — the latter playing an especially critical role. There are also significant differences. Jazz relies on the art of improvisation. The composer provides a foundation for the melody and harmonies, and the performers improvise on that. Thus, every performance of "Blue in Green" will be different.

In terms of musical structure, the piece does not rely on the major-minor system; it emphasizes modes. Modes are similar to the scales underlying the major-minor system, but they generate a different palate of harmonies. Furthermore, the harmonies in jazz are a bit more ambiguous than they are in classical music from the common practice period.

A nonmusician might look at it this way: classical music of the common practice period structures the harmonies, almost exclusively, as though constructing a three- or four-story building. Jazz harmonies are more like an eight-story building — more pitches stacked on top of one another. It is a bit harder for the nonmusician listener to immediately discern which sound is from the foundation of the building and which from one of the upper stories. I liken the effect, as it appears in "Blue in Green," to one of floating on a calm lake. The recording begins with piano and string bass, the piano softly offering the melody and harmonies in the middle register of the instrument. A muted trumpet then plays the melody (a mute is a device put in the bell end of the instrument to soften its sound), with piano, bass, and drums playing calmly in the background. The trumpet's slow-moving, wistful melody seemingly floats on top of the piano, bass, and drums. But this melody is different in structure compared with the two Beethoven works: it contains more of the larger intervals, therefore it sounds a bit more jagged.

When the trumpet plays higher notes, tension rises, but then quickly subsides as the trumpet moves to lower pitches. The drums in the background (which often provide beat and momentum in other pieces) are played here with brushes rather than drumsticks, so the sound is more like a calm breeze. The saxophone enters at 2:30, a sound similar to that of the muted trumpet, which is now silent. The higher pitches on the saxophone create tension too, of course. The trumpet next reenters, the saxophone now silent, as though the two are having a conversation, each improvising on the fundamental melody.

Aside from the brief sections where the piano has the main theme, I think of the sonority of piano, bass, and drums combined as representing the Vietnam Veterans Memorial, while the solos of trumpet and saxophone designate two friends, say, who visit the memorial together. The atmosphere of calm harmonies and relaxed tempo — though brief moments of tension are created for both trumpet and saxophone — are the prompts for sublime sadness. By the phrase "calm harmonies" I mean slower harmonic rhythm (see above), a preponderance of major-quality chords, or both.

The folk hymn, "**Amazing Grace**," (Piece 1.24) has a long history. The poem was written in the late eighteenth century. It was subsequently sung to at least two dozen different melodies before it stuck, more than fifty years after its creation, to the melody it has been sung to ever since. "Amazing Grace" can be sung as a solo, without any accompaniment, or as a four-voice hymn. Later composers, however, have expanded on the essence of the original folk hymn considerably, even for a full orchestra or large band.

What is always the centerpiece, though, is the melody. Like most folk songs, it has a narrow pitch range (in this case, one octave), so most people can sing it. The rhythms are simple — most notes last one or two beats — but the quicker notes (such as those sung on the syllable *zing* in *amazing*) imbue the melody, which could have been otherwise a plodding hymn, with an artistic twist, at the beginning, end, and twice in between, creating symmetry. This shape of the melody is mesmerizing, having its beginning in a low vocal register, then, midway, working its way to its highest, now falling back again — roughly like a large arch, slowly and gently pulling the listener to the peak, then gradually descending (not unlike the Vietnam Veterans Memorial).

This melody, like the original poem, is divided into phrases. Another way of saying this is that the melody has commas and periods, allowing the listener moments of repose along the arch. Although the rising portion of the arch incites momentum, its tempo is slow: the melody never fails the purpose of calmness. Finally, unlike a Beethoven symphony or a jazz piece, where most in the audience will never have acquired the skills needed to perform the work they are listening to, "Amazing Grace" is singable by nearly everyone — a parallel to it becoming so easily embedded into the memory of nearly anyone listening.

"Don't Think Twice, It's All Right," performed by Bob Dylan (Piece 1.2), gives us a very different musical angle on sublime sadness.[7] The tempo is quicker than in any of the works we have discussed thus far, and the guitar provides constant momentum. But comparing the momentum in the guitar to the vocalist's melody, the latter holds us back: it has commas and periods, just like the text, providing snippets of repose. The repetition in the guitar and vocal lines is calming: the listener knows what's coming. The very few high, or tense, pitches in vocal line are offset by an otherwise calm vocal register.

That relative absence of tension is amplified by the vocalist speaking, rather than singing, the phrase "it's all right," ending each of the four stanzas. Given the vocalist's singing register by comparison to his speaking register, "it's all right" is in the calmest register of all, almost like a forgiving sigh — loss is acknowledged, so nothing blocks its prompting sublime sadness. The harmonica interludes mimic what has already been discussed: they are a substitute for the vocal lines. The lyrics contain some poignant phrases, such as, "I gave her my heart but she wanted my soul." But any finger-pointing in the text is offset by Dylan's feeling within the phrase "it's all right."

How well do my suggestions work for identifying music likely to prompt a listener to feel sublimely sad?

Let me put them to a test during an examination of the second movement (Adagio) of the Dvořák cello concerto (Piece 1.10). This movement has me feeling natural grief — sublime sadness — immediately with its opening measures. It's an orchestral section exhibiting all eight musical traits I've discussed (see table 3.1): a slow, quiet, fairly simple music with a calm, nearly hymnlike melody.

Table 3.1.

Eight contributing traits within the musical evocation of sublime sadness

Musical trait	**Evocative of sublime sadness**
Momentum	Calm (slow)
Tempo	Slow
Melodic rhythm	Slow
Harmonic rhythm	Slow
Texture	Simple
Melodic intervals	Small (seconds, thirds, fourths)
Dynamics	Restrained (often soft)
Register	Low or middle range

Its phrasings remind me of sentences that contain pauses caused by commas and periods. Soon the solo cello enters, repeating the opening melody — mostly in the middle register of the instrument. No member within the table of eight has disappeared. At 2:03 comes a section evoking another affect altogether — anguish. The composer has inserted a chord known as fully diminished, which has a history of arousing distress beginning in the Baroque.[8] And, by comparison with the opening section, here the cello line moves faster, is played in its upper register, and is forte. Four within the table of eight traits underlying the sublime have disappeared. At 2:20, the cello's line dissolves into a series of sobs and sighs,[9] the register gradually going lower and lower and the sobs quieter and quieter. At 2:33 a flute enters with a high melody above the cello; the other seven traits within the table have returned, though, signaling a return to the sublime.

Representative sections evocative of mournfulness-anguish-distress recur at 3:08 and 4:23. They each contain three traits only from the table of eight. Representative sections evocative of sublime sadness recur at 3:45, 5:18, and 6:32. Each contains five or more traits, and a section at 6:32 evokes a sense of being suspended between these two affective poles; it contains four of the table's eight. I rest my case.

NOTES

1. Editor's Note. Dr. Pickett is keenly aware that a history of curiosity and commentary pertinent to the relationships between musical structure and the affects music evokes extends over many centuries, beginning in the ancient world and going on still in the work of currently active scholars and researchers. For this chapter, however, because our concern is for a highly specific affect that we co-authors are taking pains to define and illustrate, Pickett will forego a historical review.
2. It has been speculated that these vocal melodies may have been accompanied by instruments, but since their music was not written down, speculation must suffice.
3. Phone conversations with Susan Pickett, 2019.
4. Rhythm is defined as the distribution of durations (of notes).

5. Well, the determinants of momentum (tempo and rhythm — for the latter, both melodic and harmonic) are written, but the interpretation of what's written — thereby the creation of momentum, as well as dynamics — is, of course, an aspect of performance.
6. In this chapter, when a specification of time elapsed within a piece is mentioned, it's based on the recording suggested in Chapter I or II. If you are listening to a different recording, interpret my specification of time as an estimate, one that may differ from your own measurement by as many as 20 seconds.
7. To appreciate my comments about this piece, the reader will want to choose, if not the recording suggested in Chapter I, at the least one in which Dylan himself is the performer.
8. Much later, it became a go-to chord for just this purpose in music written for silent films.
9. The sense of a person's sigh is evoked by a falling second interval in the melody, followed by a rest or some other melodic device that creates a pause. The term "a Mozart sigh" (*Seufzermotiv*) has even been coined.

CHAPTER V

Art and Easing the Suffering of Loss:
In Everyday Life and within Psychotherapy

ROBERT ARNOLD JOHNSON

Would any, save a madman, tell a mother not to weep at the burial of her son? At such a time as that, 'twere foolish to talk of resignation. When she has given full rein to her grief, and eased the burden of her affliction, then is the time, with words of consolation, to try to soften the blow. The art of medicine, one may almost say, is the art of choosing the moment to intervene. — Ovid, 18 BCE[1]

THE FOLLOWING is a comment in print about grief that I and my coauthors might be expected to attack: "Grief is a very personal process; everyone has his or her own way to grieve and changes to undergo during the transition."[2] But we will not attack, nor even chide. True, it is not a comment we who have written this book about the feeling of natural grief, which we believe to be universal among humans, might have written ourselves. Yet the comment captures something important about grief, both what we call natural (innate or primary) grief and the collection of reactions to loss (affective and behavioral) for which we prefer the term *mourning* but which is more widely nowadays called simply *grief*.[3] Innate grief *feels* exceedingly personal because it is sublime sadness, and nothing feels more personal than an experience of the sublime, which arouses the enigmatic realization of being uniquely individual, uniquely alive, uniquely mortal. Yet, seemingly a paradox, the feeling resides on the commons of humankind and, for this reason, is powerfully prosocial; it draws us together (see the Introduction and Chapter VI for more discussion of this point). And the collection of affects and behaviors that make up mourning, of which natural grief is just one member, is displayed, in number and in degree, so variably from person to person (even within the hourly experience of the same person) — and this on the stage of who a person is and has been beforehand, something already unique. How can we deny that a mourner's suffering is, indeed, her own?

    Nor is what I will be saying in this chapter, which declaims about the therapeutic use of evoking the essence of grief — an innate, primary affect — intended to subtract an iota from the worth of the marvelous and astonishing explosion of research, imagination, and creative effort that in the last quarter century and more has gone into the understanding of prolonged, disabling mourning. Not only do I lack evidence from controlled trials for the efficacy of what I am about to suggest, I lack personal experience with a great many, nearly all, among the dazzling (even dizzying) array of therapeutic techniques brought forward during this new enrichment.[4] So I will couch what I have to contribute within a series of contexts, and within those, I will do my best to be clear about where my experience and practice lie and where they do not.

As for a matter of belief(s), I wish to be clear also: I am a physician. I believe in the medical model in those circumstances in which I am charged with caring for a person's distress that is reasonably considered an aspect or result of a disordered condition, an illness. I believe in the power of diagnoses and treatments based on them, the latter evidence-based whenever possible and judgment-based (mine and my patient's collaboratively) when it is not. Not every distress, however, brought to my attention by someone under my care is a matter of, or a result of, illness. Distress may be, even when pronounced, simply an aspect of living, of health, wherein the medical model is moot.[5] I hold, contrary to some, that a physician can be a friend instead, in such instances, but in a qualified way. She may, and often should, listen, and listen empathically,[6] but she should not advise, as friends often do; she may suggest, however, that her friend seek advice from other friends, family, or qualified authorities, as the case may dictate. Mourning of the many losses we each must endure, added up in its every degree, is more frequently and consciously experienced in health, I suspect, than is love. Yet, and perhaps for that reason, it may slip — as if by the weight of it all and the vulnerability of its host — into a matter of illness.

Entrusting the medical model — the concept of illness — to account for suffering and disability resulting from a universal and frequent experience, that of loss, based on the extreme severity of the reactions to it, is a cultural decision, quite obviously.[7] We might instead have continued to be satisfied with locutions like, "Well, he was just so, so heartbroken, he killed himself a month after she died." As an official declaration, that trust is recent, thanks to those among the very contributors to this new explosion of interest in mourning who have worked tirelessly to bring this declaration about. I am grateful for their effort and their success. I will not single them out here except to mention the one who has touched me most. She is Katherine Shear, the principal investigator for an elegantly conceived, carefully executed, clinical trial testing the efficacy of a hybrid psychotherapy that she helped design to treat prolonged, intractable mourning.[8] Bereavement was the form of loss in each subject selected; each was assigned randomly to either this new, special therapy or to a well-validated therapy for depression. The special therapy wins out: it is twice as effective as the depression therapy in this population of the severely bereaved, though Shear and coworkers remind us that their treatment still relieves the condition it's designed for in only half of the sufferers. One may quibble over some of the trial's features and presumptions, but it demonstrates conclusively, to my mind, that prolonged mourning has a being, an ontological status, of its own; it is not simply a variant of depression, even though depression is commonly one of its constituents, and when it is, further relief beyond that provided by mourning-specific psychotherapy alone will likely take place if antidepressant medication is added.[9]

Yet putting the medical model to use for framing the extreme version of what I might prefer to call *defensive triumph* over natural grief (see Introduction) is not the only lasting contribution, in my opinion, to come from the wave of clinical researchers of this newest century.[10] Again, I will single out only one such contribution from those I most admire, one that takes the form of an impassioned argument for seizing upon its point of view about a condition, that toxic brew of prolonged mourning, post-traumatic stress disorder (PTSD), moral injury, and self-assault so often experienced by veterans of military service, a condition that has almost wholly defeated, to date at least, the medical model for its relief. This argument, authored by Kate Dahlstedt, has this central point, for me a revelation: healing the returning soldier's distress should be, perhaps must be, carried out with the active help of the community the soldier comes from.[11] And by community, Dahlstedt does not mean mainly a collection of local veterans; she means representatives of the soldier's fellow citizenry.[12] She credits the earlier work and thought of Edward Tick as the inspiration for her own;[13] reading Tick's work myself, I can see why. I will add that Elizabeth Samet's recent publication on the terrors of war, *Looking for the Good War*, cited in our Introduction, served for me as excellent preparation for grasping why Dahlstedt and Tick may so plausibly and justifiably take on, as they surely do, the voice of insistence.

Why does defensive triumph over natural grief reach the extremity that it does, and thereby create the havoc that it does, in the lives of some persons by comparison with others? Where death is the source of loss, sufficient research and thought is published to believe that explanatory factors lie in two dimensions. One has to do with how and under what circumstances death happened for the person who is the object of bereavement. The other has to do with the person who is bereaved. In the first dimension are these observations. Prolonged and disabling mourning is more likely if,

(1) the death is inflicted violently (homicide or suicide or a mortal accident); if,
(2) it is by natural means but is either sudden and unexpected or happens in-hospital rather than at home; if,
(3) it is that of an intimately connected person, most especially that of a child of the bereaved; or if,
(4) it takes place within a circumstance wherein the bereaved is made to feel alone, or worse, must feel herself dismissed or the object of contempt.

The other dimension, that of the bereaved person's capability for bearing the stress of loss, is commonly and fruitfully these days explored in the language of attachment theory,[14] supplemented by careful attention to the place of meaning-making within a self-conception.[15] My own preference, though, having to do with the particularities and peculiarities of my training and interests, favors an especially clinical language of identity that sustains a concept of personality organization,[16] and it will become evident as I highlight my approach in structuring treatment for mourning — if and when mourning requires treatment. Where it doesn't, or when I'm not the one to deliver it, I will have something to say, too, something about my habits, preferences, and suggestions for giving comfort for its own sake.

Sublime Sadness and Art to Evoke It: Context Is Everything

Among the most serious, yet common, of all questions, I

believe, is this one: How to comfort a person who's mournful? The question is raised by people generally, of course, those who want to be helpful, or at least not a nuisance. Yet it comes up even in the minds of psychotherapists — if I may be taken as an example — not so much, to state the obvious, when they sit with a mournful patient and may apply a carefully established point of view and their considerable experience, but in their life out of the office, when they have not been engaged as a therapist. What to do, how to be, then? So, context is everywhere weighty, bearing on the matter not only of if and when to spotlight sublime sadness, but on the larger matter it's contained within — just how may one be of comfort? And how does that depend on its setting?

A friend shares a loss. If and when a friend brings mourning to me as a matter to be shared, wholly divorced from any engagement of me as a therapist or adviser, I'd have myself simply say, "Please, tell me more," and I'd listen. Thomas Davis's ultrabrief and poignant model for listening is never far from my mind,[17] nor is Salman Akhtar's putting the adjective *credulous* before the noun (gerund) *listening*.[18] By now I am so practiced in hearing stories of loss I very soon find myself feeling sublime sadness, whether or not that affect is within the awareness of my friend, and in that moment, if there is just enough natural pause in the transmission, I say, "I'm so sorry!" One reason I impose on myself this bit of delay in saying something so obvious is that, by saying it when I'm under the spell of innate grief, it will be felt by my friend, instantly, to be empathic: it's thereby an aid to the friend's finding their way to this soothing, sad feeling too. For those less practiced, I don't suggest the delay: instead, say "I'm so sorry" as soon as you detect that it's a matter of loss that your friend is sharing. Yes, it's more the idea of sorrow than the feeling of it that you transmit, but that too is heard, usually, as supportive. It's the listening, anyway, that counts most. If the friend is a close one, I make sure on our parting that we have set up a time to meet soon for more talk — their talk, my listening — unless the friend has given me some signal that privacy is a priority for them, in which case I make a mental note to call on my own initiative within the next few days.

A friend asks advice about mourning. Let's presume here that the foregoing — having to do with listening, empathy, and my availability — has already taken place. If the friend is a close one and the loss is very acute, especially if it involves the death of a loved one — within the week, say — I put to use what I'm likely to know already about the religious and social supports that lie within my friend's everyday traditions and preferences, and I make suggestions.

For example, if my friend is Jewish and at least potentially observant, I'll speak favorably toward sitting shivah (see Introduction). If my friend is either nonreligious or of a religion without a ritual for mourning, I may suggest a few days off work, staying at home — with spouse, if married and if both have a cooperative employment — and ensuring that those closest and available (myself included) know they are welcome to drop by; they are wanted. It's a suggestion for a gentile's make-do shivah (though I don't mention the matter of the rent garment). I think alcohol should be avoided or severely limited during this time, even by those of us who are daily wine drinkers. Abstinence, in other words, whether relative or absolute, is part of this make-do ritualistic observance.

And, yes, I suggest further, even (or especially) at this time, that my friend set aside two or three pairing periods daily — five to twenty minutes each, for example, of sitting, either alone or with those most sympathetic to the friend's tastes, with a memento of the deceased (a transitional object of grief) together with some favorite piece of art, one that is personally evocative of sublime sadness (music is easiest, or a poem, if with one or more friends). As a close friend, I may even know beforehand what piece or pieces of art will likely be chosen.

I believe in the funeral service. I will inquire in this regard, if such an inquiry fits the circumstance.[19] Once this make-do interval is complete, both friend and spouse should return to work. Pairing periods should continue. My friend may expect to feel less drawn to festive social occasions for a while, and that feeling, I'd suggest, is to be honored: turn down such invitations. Those closest to the bereaved will understand; if they don't, turn them down anyway. Within one to three months, though, my friend is likely to feel more receptive to festivity; if not, some thought toward professional counseling, certainly for talking things out with his physician, is appropriate.[20] Ditto for symptoms of depression, especially if thoughts of the deceased produce anguish of piercing intensity or if avoidances, mental or physical, are of much prominence. I make myself available, if asked, not for the counseling itself, but for an opinion about who might be right for my friend in that role.

My patient reports loss, mourning, or both — past or present — but I am not the therapist. This is a common event in any clinician's practice. Let's say, for example, that I am the patient's psychiatrist for the purpose of diagnosis, pharmacotherapy, and coordinating care with overall case management, but in this case, the psychotherapy is provided by another clinician. I begin just as with a friend who is sharing — not one asking advice — and along the way I inquire about my patient's schedule of psychotherapy. Does the therapist know about the information being confided to me? If I have the impression that my patient's experience of mourning to date is nearly or wholly dominated by defensive triumph over sublime sadness, I go the next step, does an internist or family physician know? Would my patient mind if I call both the therapist and the physician to ensure that we caregivers are well coordinated during this period of mourning?[21] Almost always the answer to this last question is, "Yes, that's fine — it's a good idea. Thank you!"

I want very much to avoid introducing contradiction among us professionals upon whom, each one of us, the patient has conferred an alliance. I mention that mourning may sometimes interfere with the usual evenness of mood, initiative, and impulse so that if my patient comes to suspect that medication may need adjusting, or if the therapist does, then either may, of course, call me for an earlier appointment than the one currently scheduled. I inquire about suicidal thoughts, most especially if the loss suffered has been via suicide. I also advise a limitation for alcohol consumption and explain why. I do not mention *pairing periods* or artworks, though I'm frequently tempted.

On occasion, I'll be asked something to this effect: "What is the point of all this pain? Where does it lead? Does it come to anything good, or is pain the only point in life, really — if we're honest about it?" And having been asked, I answer, "Well, as in everything else, people differ in the conclusion they reach for these questions. The task of your therapy is to help you to your own conclusion, and the fact that it's your own is of considerable importance. About mine, I'll say this much. The point of pain is to face reality. Life has moments, sometimes quite long moments, of pain; it's cruel that way. By learning to bear that pain, to acknowledge it, then tolerate it, we get to see what's on the other side. We learn a deeper, more confident, trust in ourselves and our judgments. For me, one of those judgments is this: life has beauty in addition to pain; it has moments of sublime beauty. We can know that, truly, only if we too have known pain and borne it — if we've learned to distinguish reality from the illusion of it. And that's a way, maybe the only way, to be able to help others who matter to us to bear their own pain. We can't help them bear pain if we ourselves haven't done it.

And finally, where does it lead? For quite a while now, whenever I think of my mother, I smile. It's a sad smile — I miss her, yes — but the smile is not ironic or otherwise defensive; it holds pleasure — it's about her. More than pleasure, there's a beauty in my missing her, right there in my own mind (or here, however the mind can be located); it's embedded by now in who I am.[22] And for some of the others in my life, now deceased, I have that same smile, For still others, in place of a smile, there's something more like a grimace, but it's a calm one bearing a peculiar beauty of its own. With thoughts of still others, I find myself grumbling or even cursing. And I'm OK with it: there's a beauty here, too, the beauty of 'Stuff happens!' — and then I smile. I've a right to."

My patient, for whom I'm the therapist, reports loss

(or I uncover it) suffered now or in the past. Here we have a context containing contexts. At the outset, there's the clarification of loss as loss between us, patient and therapist, even if the patient's internal registry of loss as loss will be in itself a matter for therapy. This initial clarification is often mooted, of course, if the loss event is recent and, at first telling, its status of loss is very clear. At the other pole is an event from the past mentioned within a therapy session, an event that has not previously been seen as one of loss. Such occasions are, for example, common enough within sessions of prolonged exposure therapy for PTSD, during which a particular retelling of the story at the heart of the disorder prompts a new memory. Another example: a patient reflects during a psychodynamic treatment in such a way that I, the therapist, take up a thread that leads to an acknowledgement about an event, recent or long past, one that has been unidentified previously as loss but should be reconceived as such and thereby mourned.

Once loss as loss is clarified between us, next comes an assessment of the status of its mourning. Where mourning has not even commenced, I will speak to its makeup, as I conceive of it, namely, that it comprises an essence of calm sadness, which I will refer to as *essential grief*, and very, very often a "surround" of feelings and behaviors that I will refer to as defenses — anguish, anger, and avoidance (the last to include numbing, denial, and regressive helplessness) being the three most common. I discuss, briefly, viewpoints on the structure of mourning that compete with mine, and why I hold to the one I do. I mention the metaphor of loss creating a wound of the self, a painful one, within who one is, a metaphor that we will make use of repeatedly, and how extending it permits us to speak of the actual experience, feeling, of essential grief as the salve for that wound. I do not, here at the beginning, characterize the sadness of essential grief as sublime — that will come later — but simply as calm. I speak at some length about the distressing and evasive defenses and why they exist, about why I prefer the term mourning for the entirety — essential grief plus the defensive structure of its surround — and about how no one can predict beforehand just what form their mourning will take. And I speak about how resistant the defenses within mourning are to internal command, shame, disgust, or contempt. We will face them together, empathically, as feelings — very real feelings indeed — to be named, waited out, borne.[23]

And here I'll mention the propensity of distress to come in waves. Meanwhile I introduce gradually the felt experience of essential grief by making use of artworks and pairing periods, which I illustrate (I use an office speaker and a digital recording) with the introductory measures to the second movement of Dvořák's cello concerto (Piece 1.10), and by asking my patient to imagine some aspect of the loss we're speaking of. Thus begins serial inquiry over time, waiting and watching, while we two discover the form that mourning will take as it develops fully. Along the way, I will invite, where my patient's reflective capacity permits, some discussion of the meaning of death and loss (see above) and some about values as meaning. What values from the start were shared with the deceased? What values were learned from and taught to the deceased? Which, if not shared, were observed? Could those be appreciated or not? And always I'm curious about my patient's own favorite pieces of art, initiating a selection process that we may revisit indefinitely; I'll want to be sure that the pieces we select are evocative for sublime sadness for us both. By this point I will have made emphatic an opinion, my own, that a meaning of mourning resides within its essential component, the sublimity of its sadness, a meaning of meanings (see Introduction and Chapter VI).

Having clarified that loss indeed has been experienced, having established an understanding about how, in my view, mourning a loss gets structured in our minds, and having introduced the use and purpose of pairing periods, the second phase of assessment amounts to a judgment about the severity of mourning's defensive component.[24] Has it imposed extraordinary suffering, functional impairment, or both? Has, in short, a universal experience of humankind slipped into something else, an illness? I make use of the dual process model of mourning as I ponder these questions.[25] Most often the answer to each is no and remains so. I have a strong impression that the pairing periods have been a comfort — and this perhaps understates the matter — but I have no formal or informal trial-based evidence by way of confirmation.

More than one recent writer about mourning, as mourning applies to bereavement, has expressed the view that it is not a matter of resolution, recovery, or "closure," that it is, in some sense, forever. Well, yes and no. I like Wolfelt's quotation from playwright Robert Anderson: "Death ends a life; it does not end a relationship."[26] I do not view the persistence of a defensive shield within mourning as inevitable. Innately, grief is there or meant to be (more on this below), awaiting release into realization. I believe natural grief to be an affect, not a cognition —

though it facilitates cognitions — an aesthetic affect sublimely sad.[27] Where it leads, or if it does, depends most perhaps on the balance of affect one had felt for the deceased and the circumstance of their death.[28] Where love predominates for someone dying a "good enough death,"[29] natural grief is an invitation to acceptance, as I've defined it, depending on the circumstance. Where regret, distrust, or hostility dominate over love,[30] or where the death, perhaps of one's child, was certainly not "good enough," sublime sadness will do, to say the least, on its own; acceptance in such a circumstance may lie beyond the pale.

How do I go about the treatment of prolonged grief disorder (PGD)? First, still more context setting. I am a general psychiatrist for adults and older adolescents, one working within a private office and doing a good deal more psychotherapy than is usual for general psychiatrists. My special interests are disorders of mood, personality, or both, but I also look after persons referred for any psychiatric disorder whatever, so long as my role in matters of case management can be limited.[31] As is true over all too much of the nation, psychiatric inpatient beds are scarce; the nearest such facility to my practice, usually full, is seventy-five miles distant. A local crisis response team is available; its staff is well trained and cooperative. It has within its resources a "crisis house" capable of day-and-night observation and treatment — so long as I agree to be the prescriber of medication — for up to five days. The staff employed at the emergency room for our one local hospital, including social work staff, is cooperative in the care of psychiatric patients; finding an inpatient bed, when one is needed, may take days while the patient is held there, and the facility for eventual transfer may be located several hundred miles distant. Much of the time no psychiatrist colleague exists within fifty miles. Specialists in PGD are much further away still. Its treatment in my practice will reside embedded within the treatment of another psychiatric condition; a stand-alone referral for PGD is rare. I don't care much for the lingo *PGD*, for reasons I've stated, but I'll live with it; it's now mainstream.

PGD, now by official designation and definition, is an illness.[32] The medical model is therefore an appropriate model — I'll go further, *the* model — for its care for two main reasons. One is that it so often contains depression, an illness, within its makeup — something requiring diagnosis and prescription of either psychotherapy or medication, and medication is most convenient because the therapy "space" will be already taken up by a therapy focusing on PGD. The second is that features of PTSD, particularly avoidance features, are almost invariably present. PTSD is an illness too; it must be diagnosed and treated. My guess is that the reason prolonged grief disorder therapy (PGDT) proved more likely to relieve PGD than depression therapy alone in Shear's study is this: it contains exposure (imaginal) techniques that are of proven usefulness in PTSD; they are essential. (I will not herein list the defining features of PGD beyond what I've said to this point; they are enumerated in DSM-5-TR[33] and by Holly Prigerson and colleagues.[34])

So that's what I do first, initiate or adjust medication for depression and introduce intervals of imaginal exposure treatment for PTSD, of course presuming that, with one exception, what I've described in the foregoing about my approach to mourning is in place. That one exception is pairing periods. These I postpone until enough improvement has taken hold, enough relaxation of mourning's defensive shield (see the quotation from Ovid that began this chapter), for sufficient reflective capacity to be extant. The same is true for other reflection-based interventions, such as exploring a likely role of unacknowledged rage, ambivalence, or both (toward the deceased) and of fear over one's own eventual death.[35] Once I get the sense, though, that reflective capacity is beginning to emerge, pairing periods — initially in-session, then transferred to twice daily out-of-session exercises of five to thirty minutes' duration — begin. Again, my impression is that they provide an almost immediate comfort, a turn in the direction of relief, and thereby a space within which the other reflection-based features of the treatment can begin to take effect.[36]

In my practice, as I've commented, PGD is not a stand-alone psychiatric matter. The context overall most often involves some degree of personality disorder. And *personality disorder* is the language I prefer for my own use, over *attachment disorder* or *attachment style*, because it merges seamlessly with choice among an array of evidence-based psychotherapies.[37] Of these I make use more of transference-focused psychotherapy (TFP) than any other,[38] as it makes the best fit with the resources available to me by virtue of my own training and those within the community in which my practice resides. A therapy for personality disorder takes a while — one to three years, minimum, of weekly or, better yet, twice weekly, sessions. It accommodates a concomitant therapy for PGD of the type I'm describing. In the most severe cases of personality disorder, or in those enchained within an impoverished circumstance or a microculture otherwise inhibitory for, or hostile toward, treatment, the disorder does not relent, and most especially if antisocial features have an important part. Yet in a majority it does relent or considerably improve, and in those cases, PGD remits also, provided it has been adequately addressed.

"Meaning-making," as a goal within the treatment of PGD, a goal thought to be important by several contemporary clinician-scholars contributing to its literature, resides within three parts of the treatment I describe here. First, there is the values-as-meaning aspect of the model for mourning that I propose and discuss with the patient initially. Second, there is that contained within the dynamically focused, inescapably existential (and phenomenological) aspect of exploring unacknowledged perceptions of the deceased, as well as unacknowledged phobia attached to death itself. And third, far more direct, is the experience, repeatedly, of sublime sadness — natural grief. And for the sublime's meaning, we have more to say.

NOTES

1. Excerpted from "Love's Cure" in *Love Books of Ovid*, 188, translated from the Latin verses into English prose by J. Lewis May in 1930 for a private printing by Rarity Press. The re-edition of this work I've used here is published under the title *The Love Books of Ovid Being the Amores, Ars Amatoria, Remedia Amoris and Medicamina Faciei Femineae of Publius Ovidius Naso* by Kessinger's Rare Reprints.
2. Li and Chang, "Grief Healing Garden," 241.
3. A precedent for preferring the term mourning for this purpose and in this sense can be found in Fallon, "Interrupted Mourning," 189. And a precedent for Fallon is the extended argument to the same end presented by Bowlby, *Loss*, 18–19.
4. See, just for example, collations of techniques within the two books

edited or co-edited by Robert Neimeyer, each intended principally for specialists in treating prolonged mourning (Techniques of Grief Therapy; Grief and the Expressive Arts); also, the book by Salman Akhtar, intended for psychoanalysts (Three Faces of Mourning).
5. See Akhtar, Matters of Life and Death, 108.
6. By *empathy*, I mean an observer's subjective register of another's affect and, simultaneously, the internal recognition that it is the affect of another that she feels; thus the empathic observer feels an affect transmitted to her from another, yet maintains it as an object that she may continue to observe; she, in short, resists wholly identifying with it. I go into this, perhaps overmuch, because it seems to me so easily and often misunderstood.
7. I hardly need say that my phrase "cultural decision" is not to imply unanimity. A measured summary for opposing an application of the medical model for any aspect of mourning is presented by Wilson, *Supporting People*, 37-47. Much as I admire Wilson's expertise and thoughtfulness in the main, however, I cannot agree with his conclusion in this specific instance.
8. See Shear et al., "Treatment of Complicated Grief" (2005). Its stratagems and techniques were drawn from three therapeutic venues: some from imaginal exposure treatment for post-traumatic stress disorder (PTSD) (in this case principally aimed at the avoidance defenses so often prominent in those with prolonged mourning); some from interpersonal psychotherapy for depression; and some from a useful theoretical construct for mourning called the *dual process model* (see Zech, "Dual Process Model"). At the time of publication of the results of the trial (2005), this special, hybrid treatment was called *complicated grief therapy*, but the term *complicated grief* itself has since fallen out of common use; in the *Diagnostic and Statistical Manual of Mental Disorders*, 5th ed., text revision (DSM-5-TR), prolonged, disabling mourning is given the label prolonged grief disorder. Shear and other researchers in this field now prefer, for the name of the therapy reported on in 2005 and now widely promoted, *prolonged grief disorder therapy* (PGDT).
9. Shear et al., "Optimizing Treatment of Complicated Grief" (2016); for a list of trials since, see Simon and Shear, "Prolonged Grief Disorder" (2024).
10. This wave of research and researchers is not something arising de novo. As an introduction, see John Bowlby's now classic text, *Loss*, as

well as the two books I cite written or edited by Salman Akhtar, Matters of Life and Death and Three Faces of Mourning, the latter making up a compendium, from one psychoanalyst's perspective, of writings — poetic, philosophical, and psychological. What I mean to designate "a new wave" is a still more recent blooming of clinical scholars, one publishing about prolonged, disabling mourning and, as a result, the advent from their efforts of a new kind of practitioner, one who may be called a specialist for the treatment of this (now official) disorder.

11. See Dahlstedt, "Soldier's Heart," 233–36.
12. The program is carried out by Dahlstedt and colleagues via retreats in which afflicted soldiers, other local veterans, local civilians, and therapists are participants together; storytelling and other expressive arts are an important component. The civilian participants are crucial. This treatment bears comparison with the principles informing recent innovations for the treatment of somewhat more confined instances of moral injury, wherein a distinct role for "civilian" participants by comparison with therapists is emerging (see Svoboda, "Invisible Epidemic").
13. Tick, *War and the Soul*.
14. Shear, "Grief Is a Form of Love." Bowlby, *Loss*, 38–41. Wilson, *Supporting People*, 67-82.
15. See Thompson and Neimeyer, *Grief and the Expressive Arts*. Also Neimeyer, "Meaning of Loss Codebook," "Grief and Meaning Reconstruction Inventory," and "Perceived Life Significance Scale," chaps. 8, 9, and 11 in *Techniques of Grief Therapy*.
16. See Clarkin, Yeomans, and Kernberg, *Psychotherapy for Borderline Personality*.
17. Johnson and Davis, "Philosopher: Coda," chap. 14 in *Story by Story*.
18. Akhtar, Matters of Life and Death, 109.
19. By *funeral* I mean an occasion where people who cared about the deceased and care now about the bereaved gather to mourn together with the latter (I'm indifferent about how the deceased is presented, i.e., open casket or closed, or presented at all) — gather to mourn, that is, a death, not "celebrate" a life. If the deceased was religious, a church, chapel, temple, synagogue, prayer room, or other specified meeting place of that religion, of course, should be the setting; otherwise, it may be set in any secular assembly hall that suits the number of likely attendees, a mood of solemnity, and the presentation of music.

Some portion of the music should be chosen to evoke sublime sadness, whatever its content: religious music that evokes natural grief will fit into a secular setting as well as it does into an overtly religious one — listeners will "hear" the feeling evoked within them and ignore content that does not fit their own religious or secular preference. Why a funeral? "To every thing there is a season: . . . A time to weep, and a time to laugh; a time to mourn, and a time to dance." (Eccles. 3:1–4, Authorized Version.)

20. And have a look at other clues to "stuck" mourning that Salman Akhtar spells out in *Matters of Life and Death*, 107–8.
21. I'm implying here an action I make routinely. I wish that were more a fact than it is in truth. I fail as often, I'd guess, as I succeed.
22. Consider this quote from Alan Wolfelt: "While we can learn to reconcile ourselves to it, grief is transformative and life-changing." (Wolfelt, *Companioning the Bereaved*, 8.) Our book and this chapter within it certainly take no issue with the clause following the comma. What we mean by natural grief is something transformative; we become deepened and more complex through the experience of it. But the clause preceding the comma, from our standpoint, tempts misunderstanding. Innate grief is not a feeling to "reconcile," as if we were completing a negotiation. It is a gift from nature herself; its essence is aesthetic — beyond, or apart from, cognition (it requires no learning) — the sublime, inseparable from sadness.
23. I'm a fan of all three of the terms for this intervention that I know about: "holding" (Slochower, "Analytic Holding Environment"), "witnessing" (Akhtar, *Matters of Life and Death*, 108), and "companioning" (Wolfelt, *Companioning the Bereaved*).
24. From John Bowlby: "The suggestion I made is that defensive processes are a regular constituent of mourning at every age and that what constitutes pathology is not their occurrence but the forms they take and especially the degree to which they are reversible." (Bowlby, *Loss*, 21.)
25. The dual process model posits that mourning is two problems in one and that alternating attention toward them is typical. There is the matter of feeling the loss, of affects connected with it, on the one hand, and the matter of putting one's life back together, holding it together, on the other — coping with the implications, sometimes quite quotidian and practical, for example, of a deceased's absence from the family and home. See Shear et al., "Treatment of Complicated Grief" (2005), and

also Zech, "Dual Process Model."
26. Wolfelt, *Companioning the Bereaved*, 7.
27. Here I must depart from John Bowlby, who states: "All who have discussed the nature of the processes in healthy mourning are agreed that amongst other things they effect, in some degree at least, a withdrawal of emotional investment in the lost person and that they prepare for making a relationship with a new one." (Bowlby, *Loss*, 25.) My position is that healthy mourning leads not to withdrawal of "emotional investment" but to substitution for the old investment, the fraction of it that was dependence-based, with a new emotion: sublime sadness. And this substitution tracks a shift of locating: a personhood once located in the world to a personhood located now in the bereaved's mind. Once the new location is secured, acceptance may unfold.
28. See the discussion, much of it within an endnote, of whether essential grief "leads to" dawning hope or acceptance in Chap. I, Piece 1.23.
29. Akhtar, *Matters of Life and Death*, 109–12.
30. This conception, and this locution for it, I've learned from Salman Akhtar during his informal talks with residents in psychiatry at Thomas Jefferson University Hospital, Philadelphia, 2004–7.
31. I do not treat military veterans suffering from PTSD — see my commentary about the work and writings of Kate Dahlstedt and Edward Tick above — because none are referred: a VA Medical Center exists within my community. Also, I saw no such patients during my residency in psychiatry. In short then, I have no personal experience bearing on their condition, though I do bear a great deal of empathy for the suffering it imposes, suffering very possibly beyond the scope of a medical model for comprehending. I take some comfort, though, from what I've learned from the authors I've cited already.
32. DSM-5-TR, 322.
33. *Diagnostic and Statistical Manual of Mental Disorders*, 5th ed., text revision.
34. Prigerson, Shear, and Reynolds. "Prolonged Grief Disorder Diagnostic Criteria." See their "PG-13-Revised" checklist. I do regret that "sorrow" is included within this checklist as an example of "emotional pain" and thereby becomes enwrapped within a concept of illness. Surely, we might expect more specificity for illness than the word sorrow conveys.
35. Akhtar, *Matters of Life and Death*, 109, 112–18.
36. I am enthusiastic about the literature bearing on the treatment of PGD

by engagement in expressive arts (see Thompson and Neimeyer, *Grief and the Expressive Arts*; also, McNiff, *Integrating the Arts*). Were specialists of this kind available to me, I would add them to my treatment plan via referral; alas, they are not.

37. I have expressed elsewhere my view of the term personality disorder and its definition. See Johnson and Davis, "Flauta's Notes" and "Psychiatrist: Account and Applications," chaps. 6 and 8 in *Story by Story*.

38. TFP is a psychodynamic treatment for personality disorder designed by Otto Kernberg, Frank Yeomans, John Clarkin, and their colleagues in New York and validated for effectiveness by randomized trial. It makes use of psychoanalytic principles, specifically those derived from object-relations theory, but as a vehicle for them it differs in several important ways from psychoanalysis. The therapist sits facing a sitting patient; the sessions are twice weekly rather than daily; the therapist is quite actively interventional (clarifying, interpreting) by comparison with an analyst; the therapy begins with an extended "contract setting" that specifies boundaries for behavior and a must-follow strategy for what to do about suicidal thinking. See Clarkin, Yeomans, and Kernberg, *Psychotherapy for Borderline Personality*; also, Yeomans, Clarkin and Kernberg, *Transference-Focused Psychotherapy*.

CHAPTER VI

The Oneness of Grief and the Sublime:
An Elaboration

ROBERT ARNOLD JOHNSON

THIS WORD *sublime*: why not *beauty* instead? Our answer is this: *beauty* is too generic for our purpose. Consider the word as defined by George Santayana:[1] "Beauty is pleasure regarded as the quality of a thing... a value... an emotion.... Beauty is an ultimate good.... It is pleasure objectified." We want more specificity than the word *beauty* provides; we want that poignant affect, frequently abrupt, sometimes breath-catching, so often bursting into, "Oh, *how* beautiful!" We want to specify one species of beauty, in short, the one some might call *ravishing*, others, *the sublime*. The following expression, taken from a well-known work of Hans Küng,[2] works for us, although the author himself put it to a slightly different purpose: "the still hidden, incomprehensibly great mystery in us and around us." Of the same character is this quotation from John Dewey: "the mystic aspect of acute aesthetic surrender."[3] Or this one from *The New Yorker*'s Peter Schjeldahl: "the irresponsible joy of aesthetic experience."[4] Friedrich von Schiller, in a celebrated essay of 1801, defined *sublime* in a satisfying way for many of us in generations to come:[5]

> "The feeling of the sublime is a mixed feeling.... It is a composition of melancholy... and of joyousness which can mount to rapture.... By means of the feeling for the sublime, therefore, we discover that... we possess a principle proper to ourselves that is independent of all sensuous affects.... Thus Nature has even employed a sensuous means of teaching us that we are more than merely sensuous.... Most exalted inspiration of human nature! — to transfer actual suffering into sublime emotion."

I'd point especially to three things in Schiller's account. First, how closely he comes to defining, via his sense of the sublime, what we herein call *natural grief*.[6] Second, how insightfully, we may think, he interprets the source for the "joyousness," the "rapture," of the sublime: it satisfies a less conscious hunger within the mind. The argument, then, goes thus: the joy, the experience, of the sublime may be understood as the correlate of deep self-affirmation, an affirmation prompted by a sudden realization that I, bearing a sensuous experience, am doing so through my own will — I am submitting to it *by my own decision* — I am not its victim, I am its host![7]

Finally, how he dares this self-contradiction: that nature on the one hand stands down, apart, from our will and on the other is the origin for the (sublime) feeling by which we learn that fact. Some will object that the word sublime is, in modern parlance, too often seen as expressing aesthetic ecstasy to be deployable still in the context of grief. Well, these two poles, if you will, of the sublime were visualized by Schiller, too. Even in the few passages I've quoted, one will hear him veer toward the ecstatic. He left implicit something perhaps better made explicit: the sublime contains these two dimensions, (natural) grief and ecstasy.[8] After his premature death (age 46), one of his fans, Ludwig van Beethoven, in 1824 captured each of the two dimensions in his great ninth symphony: innate grief in its arresting, wondrous third movement; ecstasy in "Ode to Joy," its glorious fourth.[9]

The psychological formula by which Schiller explains why we feel the sublime did not go unnoticed. I believe it informs — as agonist for some, antagonist for others — the entire existential school of writers that will mature more than a century later. My favorite examples among the many, many possible are Albert Camus's novel *The Stranger* (1946), most especially its coda, and Victor Frankl's innovative logotherapy, brought to broad public attention in the early 1960s.[10]

One might argue even that the entire edifice of psychoanalysis, born just shy of a century after Schiller, is of a kind with the structure of his scheme for explaining the sublime. A contemporary application of it, now more than two centuries later, is evident in a New Yorker magazine piece on the painter and sculptor Bruce Nauman[11] and in a view of art expressed by a contemporary philosopher, Alex Neill.[12] This explanatory formula for the sublime rests on the notion of a human's will, her agency, an enigmatic notion because the person who's bearing it is enigmatic.[13] Natural grief, then, the sublime sadness, contains an experience of, a feeling for, enigma — and all the more when death is the loss one is grieving. That particular loss — through death — of course is special: via association one's own death is in its shadow; the life just lost, now being grieved, forecasts the inevitable — loss of oneself — enigma of enigmas. How blessed are we mortals, then, to feel the sublimity in grief?[14]

Is any experience of the sublime one of grieving? Yes. Well, one or the other, innate grief or ecstasy — the two poles within the sublime — more often an infusion of one within the other. Art is made to embody this very point.[15] That's why Schiller bothered with his famous essay. And to what end? To the end of social cohesion, a culture's cohesion.[16] That's why the Renaissance initiated for artists a promotion to the status of hero. Grief, the sublime — shared, this is a powerful prosocial feeling. Art is therefore powerfully prosocial.[17]

If you don't believe it, stand in a line (extending seemingly forever) at the Museum of Modern Art in New York City (let's say you want to get into a retrospective exhibition of Cézanne's paintings) — everyone there nearly silent, waiting, reverent — the queue itself embodying already, literally embodying, natural grief and ecstasy in anticipation. Or witness Julia Roberts's eyes in the movie *Pretty Woman* (playing Vivian, attending her first opera): they are wet, glistening, a tear or two dripping onto her cheek. Or the same rapt feeling and expression of primary grief portrayed by Cher (as Loretta) her first time at the Metropolitan Opera in the movie *Moonstruck*. Or watch an audience after an especially vivid performance of Sophocles's *Ajax*.[18]

Or consider this testament from a performance artist, Ragnar Kjartansson, who has written a piece of music called "Sorrow" for a rock band as he is being interviewed about a particular performance by the band in which the piece is played over and over for six hours (!):[19] "During the last hour, I started thinking about my daughter and completely choked up. The others took over the singing, and then the audience started — the whole room was singing." Humans must share, feelings most especially, to cohere — cohere in families, bands, tribes, cities, nations — within the cultures in which they come to speak and by and through which they survive. It's in their nature, our nature, via Nature.[20]

To feel, to bear emotion, lets me know that, as Gabriel Marcel has commented, "'This concerns me after all.' In short, it brings me back to the consciousness of my own existence."[21] Art, apprehended as such by an experience of it, provokes feeling[22] — thereby I have become aware of myself, discovered myself, recovered myself, my unique self among all possible selves — the enigma of myself. And when that feeling contains the sublime, the enigma is multifold; there is innate grief. I am conjoined into, a participant within, a community, a culture — I am not alone. Perhaps in that moment I may think the distinction between me and the source for my feeling, the distinction between subject and object, has been effaced — in an enigmatic sense they have become one — ditto for the distinction between personal and social, between the I and everyone else.[23]

Sublimity and natural grief, then — this is our belief and our message — are aspects of each other. We are not the first to notice: that took place millennia ago. Yet it seems in our day to be drastically underrecognized. Almost always my mention of it elicits surprise,[24] sometimes shock merging into outrage — true, despite some expression of the intermingled essence of these two affects being literally a part, however modest, of everyday life. Just one example, an NPR headline: "Schubert Most Sublime: The String Quintet in C"; Schubert wrote this quintet, one that has been requested by more than one distinguished musician to be played at his or her own funeral, in his last days (see the dedication to this book as well as Chapter I).

The intermingling of sublimity and sadness within primary grief is seen and unseen simultaneously in current American culture, more unseen than necessary and much more than warranted. We've wanted to make the case about the nature of grief as plain as we're able, lest the defenses — whether distressing, distracting, or numbing — that so commonly prevent or pervert our realization of it keep on getting mistaken for the thing itself, a circumstance we label as "defensive triumph." Not only does defensive triumph embed pain, anguish, or rage where calm, sublime sorrow might have been (because we perceive defensive triumph as something inevitable, inescapable, and thereby unwittingly permit it to hijack our natural vitality), but it causes us to fear what is truly inevitable — the losses we must endure in order to live — and so much more than we might otherwise.

And loss, of course, includes that which is inherent within our own finitude. But that's not all. Mistaking defensive triumph for natural grief threatens our recognition of, and thereby our experience of, sublimity itself. May anything be more disheartening toward life? For experiencing the sublime is one reason to live.[25] It answers any question about its value itself, implicitly.[26]

NOTES

1. Santayana, "The Sense of Beauty."
2. Küng, *Art and the Question*, 54.
3. Dewey, *Art as Experience*, 28.
4. Schjeldahl, "The Whitney Biennial."
5. Schiller, On the Sublime, 198–209.
6. I would insist that the calm sadness of grief is more acutely felt than the melancholy Schiller believes typical of the sublime alone (mentioned in words not quoted above): "at its utmost is manifested in a shudder" (Schiller, *On the Sublime*, 198). Yet it's true that primary, natural grief is unaccompanied by wailing, lamentation, or crying; it is calm; lachrymosity comprises wetness of the eyes, tears singly down the cheek. The more anguish- and anger-laden affects of mourning are, as explained earlier, defenses against innate grief, not the primary emotion itself.
7. Schiller is not transparent about the degree of awareness during this realization. If my own experience of it is a guide more generally, it is on the borderline of awareness, i.e., subconscious.
8. Two writers on the sublime preceding Schiller, Edmund Burke in 1756 and Immanuel Kant in 1790 (see Scruton, *Beauty*, 72–73) had emphasized *fear* within its experience. I am not thereby dissuaded from preferring *natural, primary grief*, which is closer to Schiller's *melancholy* but more precise. Burke and Kant, to my mind, have singled out awe as a stand-in for the sublime, whereas I see awe as one comember of an enigma-based triad (sublime-wonder-awe), awe being provoked less by loss than by a perceiver's *finitude* — smallness — relative to a perceived *vastness*. See the commentary about awe in Chapter I. Ben Taub's piece on the photographer Paolo Pellegrin captures the interwoven nexus of awe with sublime sadness (Taub, "In Search of the Sublime").
9. A brilliant display of the Romantic epoch's revelation — the polarity inherent within the sublime and also its role in human affairs — is on show in Darrin McMahon's "Questioning the Evidence," chap. 5 of *Happiness*, where the author makes use of quotations and examples from not only Schiller and Beethoven but also Byron and Schopenhauer — who might be considered its extremes — as well as Hölderlin, Coleridge, Wordsworth, Keats, Whitman, and Strindberg, among (if you can believe it)

others. For me, though, the final two movements of Beethoven's ninth symphony may be considered emblematic: grief and joy, each distinctly defined. In McMahon's chapter are many examples of ecstasy and innate grief, especially the latter, being confused with their defenses. Defensive triumph over sublimity might be diagnosed whenever a calm, reflective posture toward implicit enigma is wholly effaced.
10. Frankl, *Man's Search for Meaning*.
11. Schjeldahl, "Bruce Nauman's Restive Humor."
12. Neill, "Fiction and the Emotions," 272–88.
13. Again, enigmatic does not at all contradict existent. (Obviously, by composing the foregoing sentence I am forbidden to claim that logical positivism is my philosophic home.)
14. Some will feel this comment to be hopelessly Pollyannaish, even fraudulent, toward the most essential experience of humankind: the prodigious miseries of being a self, trapped in a perishable body, chief among them being a fear of inevitable death, a circumstance requiring demoralizing yet natural narcissism, plus a dependence on heroes (see Ernest Becker, *Denial of Death*, for an exhaustive exploration of this point of view). Becker is especially a champion for Søren Kierkegaard's *The Concept of Dread* (1844). A partisan to Becker's near-obsessional regard for his theme sees common defenses against death-fear (repression, denial, projection) as necessary but evil. Yet nowhere mentioned in this otherwise deeply researched magnum opus is the adaptive force of primary grief. And hope, curiosity, love, pride (not vanity), and empathy — adaptive all — get short shrift, if any. The quiet joy of productive labor, of choosing to contribute to the welfare and vitality of one's community and to individuals within it, not to speak of one's family—no or little comment. Becker's view of mental illness (variations on the theme of cowardice) is not only seriously dated, it was seriously inhumane (for me, obscenely so) even when it was current. There's something else fatally wrong with Becker's work: it leans toward an abstraction of "man," meaning the human, to a degree wherein hardly any individual person is sensible. Two-thirds of my half-century career in medicine has been as an internist-cardiologist; I have been a witness and companion to dozens of people dying. Their mood and emotion near death were so various as to defy abstraction, but natural grief was by no means rare; and it was a comfort to all — themselves, their doctors, their loved ones. Still, Becker does have marvelous insights. My favorite is in his

coda: "Life seeks to expand in an unknown direction for unknown reasons.... There is a driving force behind a mystery that we cannot understand, and it includes more than reason alone." (Ernest Becker, *Denial of Death*, 284.) Well, we cannot understand, and it includes more than reason, if we presume understanding and reason to be confined to products and process of problem-solving. A concept of enigma, though, lends sublimity to the first of Becker's two sentences, and sublimity puts question and answer into unison (see Proust, *Chardin and Rembrandt*, 21–24).

15. Often, not always, unconsciously. John Keats, to cite just one example, gave full proof that his purpose in making art was no longer locked out of his awareness, if it ever had been. See John Dewey's expression on this point about Keats's famous closing to "Ode on a Grecian Urn" (Dewey, Art as Experience, 35). And Henryk Górecki's Symphony No. 3 (*Symphony of Sorrowful Songs*), to simply cite one more example, very clearly exemplifies an artist consciously creating the sublime within grief. Yet here's a truth too: an artist consciously intending to evoke grief (and thereby the sublime) very often fails; the reason is that the artist has confused natural grief with one or more of its defenses, as so many of us do. Hence my conclusion: the sublime in art is created most often via unconscious intuition. The play of unconscious relationships and purpose may be crucial to artmaking. I do not endorse any implication that an artist's agency, intentionality, for depicting something of her experience in creating the artwork is unconscious. I am fully agreed with Flint Schier in "Van Gogh's Boots": intentionality, a conscious version, is part of what we must consider art to contain. But naming the affective quality of the experience is another matter. The intentionality of the artist goes to evoking affect, yes, one she recognizes as having been the one she wanted, most often, I think, only when she has succeeded; she knows it then, though it was nameless beforehand. Ponder this, just for example: "Art must necessarily harbor hostility towards history even greater than its aversion towards philosophy. Art inclines to be eternally young and mysterious, while history tends to make art old, and philosophy, to make it conceivable" (Mehlis, "Aesthetic Problem," 82). Fans of Julian Jaynes, among whom I count myself, will appreciate this comment about his work and thought: "Using a Jaynesian approach to view the mind's remarkable ability for unconscious processing of information,

one might speculate that the insights and intuitions which underlie most creativity and discovery in both the arts and sciences are echoes of bicamerality, 'divine dictums' no longer packaged in hallucinatory wrappings" (Morris, "Reflections on Julian Jaynes").

16. A critic of architecture, Paul Goldberger, in "A Shimmery Cube," has this comment: "One thing that science hasn't revealed yet is what creates the sublime." I think, though, we've a beginning for an evolutionary accounting of the sublime when we acknowledge its prosocial quality, as I've developed in Chapter I and will here speak to further. Awe, another enigma-induced affect that is sometimes intertwined with the sublime is posited to be an evolved affect (Christakis, *Blueprint*, 7; Keltner, *Awe*, see esp. chap. 3, "Evolution of the Soul"). And see Dewey, *Art as Experience*, 6–9, 84, and the whole of chap. 14, "Art and Civilization." Some vivid commentary on art and its prosocial purpose is present as well in Stuart Brown and Christopher Vaughan's *Play* (11, 61–62, 174), in Hans-Georg Gadamer's discussion of "festival" and the experience of art (part I, 22-53) and, emphatically, in Kant's comment that when people think aesthetically, they are "suitors for agreement" (quoted by Scruton, *Beauty*, 93). Scruton himself declares the prosocial aspect of art with admirable economy: "Implicit in our sense of beauty is the thought of community" (Scruton, 134). The same may be said for the American poet Edward Hirsch: "Poetry rises out of one solitude to meet another in recognition and connection. It companions us" (Hirsch, "Short Conversations with Poets"). Yes, by *prosocial*, as a force flowing from the experience of enigma, as in the sublime essential of grief and as evoked by some works of art, we have in mind the positive—the force of willing coherence, generosity, cooperation, empathy. This is not to deny that social coherence may also flow from works of art in a negative sense — a unification and intensification of prejudice, aggression, violence, hatred; see Ted Gioia's commentary in this regard (Gioia, *Music*, 22, in particular). Socially negative coherence, yes, may result from the *aesthetic*, taking the word at its broadest; but we do not believe that to be true of the species of the aesthetic we refer to as *sublime*. I attribute priority to Aristotle, within Western culture, for the idea that art is prosocial (*Poetics*, esp. chap. 15), although admittedly the idea is a bit between the lines of his commentary on effective technique for arousing pity and fear; still, his opposition to Plato's claim — art is distracting nonsense for social cohesion — is obvious. And the prosocial idea is not uniquely

Western: Hsun Tzu (in Cooper, *Aesthetics: The Classic Readings*, 50–54), a Chinese philosopher born nine years after Aristotle's death, makes it explicit. In our own time, Walter Goldschmidt puts the case very persuasively for there being anthropological evidence for it within indigenous cultures (Goldschmidt, "Observations," 93–114). And consider this comment by the British philosopher Roger Scruton about music and *who* one is (at the same time think of the number of people together under the spell of music, each drawn to it by this same force): "We do not hear music as we hear other sounds in our environment. Music is heard as addressed to us." (Scruton, *Music as an Art*, loc. 713 of 5017). I believe Scruton's observation is true of each artistic medium. An especially forceful case for it within the visual arts, across time and across cultures, is made by the magnificent, multi-authored tome (Careful! It weighs 7 lb.) edited by Stuart Handler, *The Commonality of Humans Through Art*. A culture's cohesion is promotional, conversely, for internal cohesion of the selves that inhabit it; see, for example, an argument made for architecture in this regard by Anthony Savile (Savile, "Architecture"). For an idea very different from, but perhaps complementary to, the prosocial one for the evolution of an aesthetic "force" within the animal kingdom see Prum, *Evolution of Beauty*.
17. And vice versa, through social means it becomes defined, made real, provided existence; see Danto, "Artworld."
18. See Mason, "You Are Not Alone Across Time."
19. See Tomkins, "Play It Again."
20. Hare and Woods, "Survival of the Friendliest," 58–63. And understand that my sentence is not made in fealty to reductionism; *Nature* is given a place within it, generically, to mean something like "all the beginning resides in *materiality and the laws governing it*, that and *enigma*." I am in wholehearted agreement with Steven Rose, who has written: "The phenomena of life are always and inexorably simultaneously about nature and nurture, and phenomena of human existence and experience are always simultaneously biological *and* social" (Rose, *Lifelines*, 279). The very same thought is captured, however inelegantly, in Robert Neimeyer and Joanne Cacciatore's phrase "epigenetic systems perspective" (Neimeyer and Cacciatore, "Developmental Theory of Grief"). I will not elaborate here a view of human evolution that best accommodates the survival-importance of "prosocial," except to say I've relied most on that of Edward O. Wilson (*The Social Conquest of Earth*).

21. Marcel, "Bergsonism and Music," 151.
22. Feeling of the enigmatic kind, something we argue here is an essential within "the aesthetic emotion," to cop a phrase from the English art critic, Clive Bell ("The Aesthetic Hypothesis," 180), and a transcultural universal. The Hindu scholar Ananda K. Coomaraswamy describes this feeling, for which the Hindi word is *rasa*, as "the very twin brother of mystic experience" (Coomaraswamy, "Dance of Śiva," 199). In claiming the existence of an aesthetically based "transcultural universal," something we do repeatedly in this book, we run afoul, we fear, of Bence Nanay's plea on behalf of "aesthetic humility" (Nanay, *Aesthetics*, 106), which would have us deny existence to any transcultural universal of an aesthetic kind. The observations he cites to make his case, though instructive and fascinating in themselves, do not persuade us to accept the necessity of his conclusion; and he nowhere takes up, let alone dismantles, evidence that might refute it. For a generalized critique of highly constructionist theories about emotion, such as Nanay's on aesthetic feeling, see Krishnan, "Cultural Influences on Emotion."
23. See Esanu, *Mimesis, Expression, Construction*, Lecture Twenty-One. In this way I can make sense of the tortured prose within the coda of this lecture about Theodor Adorno's view on art erasing the subject.
24. This comment is made respectfully and sympathetically; the defenses standing in the way of natural grief, as I've mentioned, intrude unconsciously. Some of our culture's most celebrated thinkers and writers, in discussing their own mourning, have interpreted what we herein call defenses as grieving itself. And of course, such descriptions are moving in their anguish; we are, quite rightly, condoling. See, as examples, Nussbaum, *Upheavals of Thought*, 19–33, and Naipaul, "Strangeness of Grief."
25. I do not consider this sentence to contradict Kant's celebrated admonition, first published in 1790, that we must be disinterested in something we call beautiful, meaning that it, that object to which we refer the feeling we have, must not satisfy any desire or need we have of it; it must not *gratify* (Kant, *Critique of Judgment*, loc. 643–667 of 5002). For that is the purpose of the next sentence: the sublime is a reason to live that we get without needing it; it's just there.
26. This idea, of course, is not original to me. Roger Scruton points out, for example, something of its history in his book *Beauty* (2, 191).

REFERENCES

Akhtar, Salman. *Matters of Life and Death: Psychoanalytic Reflections*. London: Karnac, 2011.

——, ed. *Three Faces of Mourning: Melancholia, Manic Defense, and Moving On*. Northvale, NJ: Jason Aronson, 2001.

——. *In Short: Private Notes of a Psychoanalyst*. London: Karnac, 2024.

Alighieri, Dante. *La Divina Commedia, Vol. I: Inferno*. Commento di Tommaso Casini. A Cura di S.A. Barbi. Sesta edizione. Firenze, Italia: G.C. Sansoni, 1979.

Almeida-Rocha, Teresa, Francisco Peixoto, Saúl Neves Jesus. "Aesthetic Development in Children, Adolescents and Young Adults." *Análise Psicológica* 1, no. 38 (2020):1–13. *https://doi.org/10.14417/ap.1657*.

Aristotle. *Poetics*. Translated by Leon Golden. Commentary by O. B. Hardison Jr. Englewood Cliffs, NJ: Prentice-Hall, 1968.

Batycka, Dorian. "Defying the Odds, Marina Abramović Presents the World Premiere of Her First-Ever Opera in Munich — Here's What It's Like." *Artnet News*, September 1, 2020. *https://news.artnet.com/art-world/marinaabramovic-1905228*.

Becker, Adam. "The Origins of Space and Time." *Scientific American*, February 2022.

Becker, Ernest. *The Denial of Death*. New York: Free Press Paperbacks, 1973.

Bell, Clive. "The Aesthetic Hypothesis." In Cooper, *Aesthetics: The Classic Readings*, 177–92.

Bowlby, John. *Loss: Sadness and Depression*. Vol. 3 of *Attachment and Loss*. New York: Basic Books, 1980.

Brown, Stuart and Christopher Vaughan. *Play: How it Shapes the Brain, Opens the Imagination, and Invigorates the Soul*. New York: Avery, 2009.

Buccellati, Giorgio and Charles Speroni, eds. *The Shape of the Past: Studies in Honor of Franklin D. Murphy*. Los Angeles: Institute of Archaeology and Office of the Chancellor, University of California, Los Angeles, 1981.

Bulfinch, Thomas. *The Age of Fable*. Vol. 1 of *The Illustrated Bulfinch's Mythology*. New York: Macmillan, 1997.

Butler, Judith. *Giving an Account of Oneself*. New York: Fordham University Press, 2005.

Calasso, Roberto. *The Marriage of Cadmus and Harmony*. Translated by Tim Parks. New York: Alfred A. Knopf, 1993.

Cavell, Stanley. "Finding Words." *London Review of Books*, February 20, 1997. *https://www.lrb.co.uk/the-paper/v19/n04/stanley-cavell/finding-words.*

Christakis, Nicholas. *Blueprint: The Evolutionary Basis of a Good Society*. New York: Little, Brown Spark, 2019.

Clarke, Eric. "Psychology of Music." In Gracyk and Kania, *The Routledge Companion to Philosophy and Music*.

Clarkin, John F., Frank E. Yeomans, and Otto F. Kernberg. *Psychotherapy for Borderline Personality: Focusing on Object Relations*. Arlington, VA: American Psychiatric Publishing, Inc., 2006.

Coomaraswamy, Ananda K. "The Dance of Śiva: Essays 3–4." In Cooper, *Aesthetics: The Classic Readings*.

Cooper, David E., ed. *Aesthetics: The Classic Readings*, 7th ed. Malden, MA: Blackwell, 2007.

Culler, Jonathan. *Literary Theory: A Very Short Introduction*. New York: Oxford University Press, 2011. Kindle.

Dahlstedt, Kate. "Soldier's Heart: Using the Arts to Heal from War." In Thompson and Neimeyer, *Grief and the Expressive Arts: Practices for Creating Meaning*.

Danto, Arthur. "The Artworld." *The Journal of Philosophy* 61, no. 19 (1964): 571–84. *https://doi.org/10.2307/2022937.*

de Bolla, Peter. *Art Matters*. Cambridge, MA: Harvard University Press, 2001.

Dennis, Thom. "The Grief River." In Neimeyer, *Techniques of Grief Therapy: Assessment and Intervention*.

Dewey, John. *Art as Experience*. New York: Berkley, 2005. Kindle.

Diagnostic and Statistical Manual of Mental Disorders, 5th ed., text revision. Arlington, VA: American Psychiatric Association, 2022.

Droitcour, Brian. "The View from Inside." *Art in America*, January 4, 2021. *https://www.artnews.com/art-in-america/features/immersive-art-1234580701/*.

Duthie, Larry. *Return to Saigon: A Memoir.* Annapolis, MD: OK-3, 2020.

Esanu, Octavian, transcriber and editor. *Mimesis, Expression, Construction: Fredric Jameson's Seminar on Aesthetic Theory*. Durham, NC: Repeater Books, recorded transcript January-April 2003, Duke University. Apple Books.

Fallon, Theodore, Jr. "Interrupted Mourning." In Akhtar, *Three Faces of Mourning: Melancholia, Manic Defense, and Moving On*.

Frankl, Viktor E. *Man's Search for Meaning: An Introduction to Logotherapy*. Boston: Beacon Press, 1962.

Freeman, Philip. *Searching for Sappho: The Lost Songs and World of the First Woman Poet*. New York: W. W. Norton, 2016. Kindle.

Freud, Sigmund. *Civilization and Its Discontents*. Translated and edited by James Strachey. Biographical introduction by Peter Gay. New York: W. W. Norton, 1961.

Gadamer, Hans-Georg. *The Enigma of Health: The Art of Healing in a Scientific Age*. Translated by Jason Gaiger and Nicholas Walker. Stanford: Stanford University Press, 1996.

——. *The Relevance of the Beautiful and Other Essays*. Translated by Nicholas Walker. Edited by Robert Bernasconi. Cambridge: Cambridge University Press, 1986.

Gates Jr., Henry Louis. *The Trials of Phillis Wheatley: America's First Black Poet and Her Encounters with the Founding Fathers*. New York: Basic Civitas Books, 2010.

Gibbons, Rachel. "The Mourning Process and Its Importance in Mental Illness: A Psychoanalytic Understanding of Psychiatric Diagnosis and Classification." *BJ Psych Advances*, vol. 30, (2023): 80-88.

Gioia, Ted. *Music: A Subversive History*. New York: Basic Books, 2019.

Goldberger, Paul. "A Shimmery Cube." *The Nation*, October 30, 2017. *https://thenation.com/article/archive//a-shimmery-cube/*.

Goldschmidt, Walter. "Observations of the Social Functions of Art." In Buccellati and Speroni, *The Shape of the Past: Studies in Honor of Franklin D. Murphy*.

Goldstein, Richard D., Carter R. Petty, Sue E. Morris, Melanie Human, Hein Odendaal, Amy J. Elliott, Deborah Tobacco, Jyoti Angal, Lucy Brink, Holly G. Prigerson. "Transitional Objects of Grief. *Comprehensive*

Psychiatry 98, no. 152161 (2020): 1–6. *https://doi.org/10.1016/j. comppsych.2020.152161.*

Goodman, Whitney. *Toxic Positivity: Keeping it Real in a World Obsessed with Being Happy.* New York: TarcherPerigee, 2022.

Gopnik, Adam. "Human Potential and the Suzuki Method." *The New Yorker*, November 14, 2022.

Gracyk, Theodore and Andrew Kania, eds. *The Routledge Companion to Philosophy and Music.* New York: Routledge, 2011.

Grant, Michael. *The Classical Greeks.* New York: Macmillan, 1989.

Handler, Stuart, ed. *The Commonality of Humans Through Art.* London: Paul Holberton Publishing, 2024.

Hare, Brian and Vanessa Woods. "Survival of the Friendliest." *Scientific American,* August 2020.

Heineman, Ben W., Jr. "Beware the Idolatry of Numbers." *The Atlantic,* August 11, 2009.

Hirsch, Edward. *Gabriel.* New York: Alfred A. Knopf, 2014.

——. "Short Conversations with Poets: Edward Hirsch." By Ilya Kaminsky. *McSweeney's,* September 10, 2020. *https://www.mcsweeneys. net/articles/edward-hirsch.*

Housen, Abigail and Philip Yenawine. *Visual Thinking Strategies: Basic Manual, Grades 3–5.* New York: Visual Understanding in Education, 2000.

Hsun Tzu. "A Discussion of Music." In Cooper, *Aesthetics: The Classic Readings.*

Hugo, Victor. *Les Misérables.* Translated by Charles E. Wilbour. New York: Modern Library, 1992.

Johnson, Robert Arnold and Thomas Alderson Davis. *Story by Story: Who I Am, What I Suffer.* Newcastle-upon-Tyne, UK: Cambridge Scholars Publishing, 2019.

Kant, Immanuel. *The Critique of Judgment.* Translated by James Creed Meredith. Dancing Unicorn eBook, 2017. Kindle.

Keltner, Dacher. *Awe: The New Science of Everyday Wonder and How It Can Transform Your Life.* New York: Penguin Press, 2023.

King, Barbara J. "The Orca's Sorrow." *Scientific American,* March 2019.

Knowles, Dudley and John Skorupski, eds. *Virtue and Taste.* Philosophical Quarterly Supplementary Series, vol. 2. Oxford, UK: Blackwell, 1993.

Konner, Melvin. *The Evolution of Childhood: Relationships, Emotion, Mind.*

Cambridge, MA: Belknap Press, 2010.

Krishnan, Nikhil. "Cultural Influences on Emotion." *The New Yorker*, August 8, 2022.

Kübler-Ross, Elisabeth. *On Death and Dying: What the Dying Have to Teach Doctors, Nurses, Clergy, and Their Own Families*. New York: Macmillan, 1969.

Kübler-Ross, Elisabeth and David Kessler. *On Grief and Grieving: Finding the Meaning of Grief Through the Five Stages of Loss*. New York: Scribner, 2014. Digital.

Küng, Hans. *Art and the Question of Meaning*. New York: Crossroad, 1980.

Lane, Anthony. "Last Laugh: Jane Austen's Final, Surprising, Unfinished Novel." *The New Yorker*, March 13, 2017.

Langer, Susanne K., ed. *Reflections on Art: A Source Book of Writings by Artists, Critics, and Philosophers*. Baltimore: Johns Hopkins Press, 1958.

Lewis, C. S. *A Grief Observed*. Introduction by Douglas H. Gresham. HarperCollins e-books. Kindle.

Li, Yu-Chan and Cypress Chang. "The Grief Healing Garden." In Thompson and Neimeyer, *Grief and the Expressive Arts: Practices for Creating Meaning*.

Libbey, Ted. "Schubert Most Sublime: The String Quartet in C," NPR, August 18, 2009. *https://www.npr.org/2011/07/18/111631425/schubert-most-sublime-the-string-quintet-in-c*.

Luzzi, Joseph. *In a Dark Wood: What Dante Taught Me About Grief, Healing, and the Mysteries of Love*. New York: Harper Perennial, 2016.

Maciejewski, Paul K. and Holly G. Prigerson. "Prolonged, but Not Complicated, Grief Is a Mental Disorder." *The British Journal of Psychiatry* 211, no. 4 (2017):189–91. *https://doi.org/10.1192/bjp.bp.116.196238*.

Marcel, Gabriel. *Being and Having*. Translated by Katherine Farrer. London: Dacre Press, 1949. Kindle.

——. "Bergsonism and Music." In Langer, *Reflections on Art: A Source Book of Writings by Artists, Critics, and Philosophers*.

Mason, Wyatt. "You Are Not Alone Across Time." *Harper's Magazine*, October 2014, 57-65.

Mayer, Elizabeth Lloyd. *Extraordinary Knowing: Science, Skepticism, and the Inexplicable Powers of the Human Mind*. New York: Bantam Dell, 2008.

McCullough, Leigh, Nat Kuhn, Stuart Andrews, Amelia Kaplan, Jonathan Wolf, and Cara Lanza Hurley. *Treating Affect Phobia: A Manual for*

Short-Term Dynamic Psychotherapy. New York: Guilford, 2003.
McMahon, Darrin M. *Happiness: A History*. New York: Grove Press, 2006.
McNiff, Shaun. *Integrating the Arts in Therapy: History, Theory, and Practice*. Springfield, IL: Charles C. Thomas, 2009.
Mehlis, Georg. "The Aesthetic Problem of Distance." In Langer, *Reflections on Art: A Source Book of Writings by Artists, Critics, and Philosophers*.
Morningstar, Barbara. *Honoring the Mystery: Uplifting Insights from the Language, Visions, and Dreams of the Dying*. British Columbia: Barbara Morningstar, 2018. Kindle.
Morris, James E. "Reflections on Julian Jaynes's The Origin of Consciousness in the Breakdown of the Bicameral Mind." In *Gods, Voices and the Bicameral Mind: The Theories of Julian Jaynes*. Edited by Marcel Kuijsten. Henderson, NV: Julian Jaynes Society, 2016.
Nagel, Thomas. *Mind and Cosmos: Why the Materialist Neo-Darwinian Conception of Nature Is Almost Certainly False*. New York: Oxford University Press, 2012.
Naipaul, V. S. "The Strangeness of Grief." *The New Yorker*, December 30, 2019.
Nanay, Bence. *Aesthetics: A Very Short Introduction*. Oxford: Oxford University Press, 2019.
Neill, Alex. "Fiction and the Emotions." In Neill and Ridley, *Arguing About Art: Contemporary Philosophical Debates*.
Neill, Alex and Aaron Ridley, eds. *Arguing About Art: Contemporary Philosophical Debates*, 3rd ed. New York: Routledge, 2008.
Neimeyer, Robert A., ed. *Techniques of Grief Therapy: Assessment and Intervention*. The Series in Death, Dying and Bereavement. New York: Routledge, 2016. Kindle.
Neimeyer, Robert A. and Joanne Cacciatore. "Toward a Developmental Theory of Grief." In Neimeyer, *Techniques of Grief Therapy: Assessment and Intervention*.
Neimeyer, Robert A. and Barbara E. Thompson. "Meaning Making and the Art of Grief Therapy." In Thompson and Neimeyer, *Grief and the Expressive Arts: Practices for Creating Meaning*.
Newman, Ira. "The Alleged Unwholesomeness of Sentimentality." In Neill and Ridley, *Arguing About Art: Contemporary Philosophical Debates*.
Nussbaum, Martha C. *Upheavals of Thought: The Intelligence of Emotions*. New York: Cambridge University Press, 2001.
O'Gieblyn, Meghan. *God Human Animal Machine*. New York: Anchor

Books, 2021.

Penrose, Roger. "The Big Bang and Its Dark-Matter Content: Whence, Whither, and Wherefore." *Foundations of Physics* 48, no. 1519 (October 2018):1177–90. *https://doi.org/10.1007/s10701-018-0162-3.*

Pieper, Josef. *Leisure: The Basis of Culture.* Translated by Gerald Marlsbary. South Bend, IN: St. Augustine Press, 1998.

Porter, Fairfield. *Art in Its Own Terms: Selected Criticism*, 1935–1975. Edited by Rackstraw Downes. New York: Taplinger, 1979.

Prigerson, Holly G., M. Katherine Shear, and Charles F. Reynolds III. "Prolonged Grief Disorder Diagnostic Criteria: Helping Those with Maladaptive Grief Responses." *JAMA Psychiatry* 79, no. 4 (February 2, 2022). *https://doi.org/10.1001/jamapsychiatry.2021.4201.*

Proust, Marcel. *Chardin and Rembrandt.* Translated by Jennie Feldman. New York: David Zwirner Books, 2016.

Prum, Richard O. *The Evolution of Beauty: How Darwin's Forgotten Theory of Mate Choice Shapes the Animal World.* New York: Doubleday, 2017.

Pugmire, David. "Sentimentality and Truthfulness." In Neill and Ridley, *Arguing About Art: Contemporary Philosophical Debates.*

Rose, Steven. Lifelines: *Biology beyond Determinism.* New York: Oxford University Press, 1997.

Rowe, William L. "Tillich's Theory of Signs and Symbols." *The Monist* 50, no. 4 (October 1966): 593–610. *https://doi.org/10.5840/monist 196650442.*

Rotterdam, Paul Z. *Nachtbogen: Nightbow and Other Events.* Munich: Hirmer, 2025.

— — . *Wild Vegetation: From Art to Nature.* Munich: Hirmer, 2014.

Samet, Elizabeth D. *Looking for the Good War: American Amnesia and the Violent Pursuit of Happiness.* New York: Farrar, Straus, and Giroux, 2021.

Santayana, George. "The Sense of Beauty." In *The Best Works of George Santayana.* Kindle.

Sapolsky, Robert M. *Determined.* New York: Penguin Press, 2023.

Sartre, Jean-Paul. *Baudelaire.* New York: New Directions, 1967. First published 1950.

Savile, Anthony. "Architecture, Formalism, and the Sense of Self." In Knowles and Skorupski, *Virtue and Taste.*

— — . "Sentimentality." In Neill and Ridley, *Arguing About Art: Contemporary Philosophical Debates.*

Schier, Flint. "Van Gogh's Boots: The Claims of Representation," In Knowles and Skorupski, *Virtue and Taste*.

Schiller, Friedrich von. *Naïve and Sentimental Poetry and On the Sublime: Two Essays*, 3rd printing. Translated by Julius A. Elias. New York: Frederick Ungar, 1980.

Schjeldahl, Peter. "Bruce Nauman's Restive Humor." *The New Yorker*, November 2, 2018.

——. "The Whitney Biennial." *The New Yorker*, May 27, 2019.

Scruton, Roger. *Beauty*. London: Oxford University Press, 2009. Kindle.

——. *Music as an Art*. London: Bloomsbury Continuum, 2018. Kindle.

Shear, M. Katherine. "Grief Is a Form of Love." In Neimeyer, *Techniques of Grief Therapy: Assessment and Intervention*.

Shear, M. Katherine, Ellen Frank, Patricia R. Houck, and Charles F. Reynolds III. "Treatment of Complicated Grief: A Randomized Controlled Trial." *JAMA* 293, no. 21 (2005): 2601–8. *https://doi.org/10.1001/jama.293.21.2601*.

Shear, M. Katherine, Charles F. Reynolds III, Naomi M. Simon, Sidney Zisook, Yuanjia Wang, Christine Mauro, Naihua Duan, Barry Lebowitz, Natalia Skritskaya. "Optimizing Treatment of Complicated Grief: A Randomized Clinical Trial." *JAMA Psychiatry* 73, no. 7 (2016): 685–94. *https://doi.org/10.1001/jamapsychiatry.2016.0892*.

Simon, Naomi M. and M. Katherine Shear, "Prolonged Grief Disorder." *New England Journal of Medicine* 391, no. 13 (2024): 1227-1236.

Slochower, Joyce. "Variations in the Analytic Holding Environment." *The International Journal of Psychoanalysis* 72, no. 4 (1991): 709–17.

Svoboda, Elizabeth. "An Invisible Epidemic." *Scientific American*, December 2022.

Taub, Ben. "In Search of the Sublime." *The New Yorker*, May 23, 2022.

Taylor, Charles. *Sources of the Self: The Making of the Modern Identity*. Cambridge, MA: Harvard University Press, 1989.

Thompson, Barbara E. and Robert A. Neimeyer, eds. *Grief and the Expressive Arts: Practices for Creating Meaning*. New York: Routledge, 2014.

Tick, Edward. *War and the Soul: Healing Our Nation's Veterans from Post-Traumatic Stress Disorder*. Wheaton, IL: Quest Books, 2005.

Tomkins, Calvin. "The Enchanter." *The New Yorker*, December 9, 2019.

——. "Play It Again: Ragnar Kjartansson and the Art of Repetition." *The New Yorker*, April 11, 2016.

Trivedi, Saam. "Resemblance Theories." In Gracyk and Kania, *The Routledge Companion to Philosophy and Music*.

Unno, Taitetsu, ed. *The Religious Philosophy of Nishitani Keiji: Encounter with Emptiness*. Nagoya, Japan: Chisokudō, 2019.

Wheatley, Phillis. *Complete Writings* (Edited and with an Introduction by Vincent Carretta). New York: Penguin Books, 2001.

Wilson, John. *Supporting People through Loss and Grief: An Introduction for Counsellors and Other Caring Practitioners*. London and Philadelphia: Jessica Kingsley Publishers, 2014.

Wilson, Edward O. *The Social Conquest of Earth*. New York: Liveright, 2012.

Wolfelt, Alan D. *Companioning the Bereaved: A Soulful Guide for Counselors and Caregivers*. Fort Collins, CO: Companion Press, 2006.

Wood, James. "Catherine Lacey and the Art of Enigma." *The New Yorker*, August 17, 2020.

Yeomans, Frank E., John F. Clarkin, and Otto F. Kernberg. *Transference-Focused Psychotherapy for Borderline Personality Disorder: A Clinical Guide*. Arlington, VA: American Psychiatric Publishing, Inc., 2015.

Zech, Emmanuelle. "The Dual Process Model in Grief Therapy." In Neimeyer, *Techniques of Grief Therapy: Assessment and Intervention*.

ABOUT THE AUTHORS

ROBERT ARNOLD JOHNSON, MD began his career as a cardiologist at the Massachusetts General Hospital and on the faculty of Harvard Medical School, where he became internationally recognized as an authority on the topic of heart failure. For reasons to do with family, he returned to the Pacific Northwest, taking up nonacademic medical practice in his early forties. At age 62, pressured by an ever more insistent intuition, he left cardiology to begin a residency in psychiatry (Thomas Jefferson University Hospital, Philadelphia — a residency providing an exceptionally emphatic psychotherapy focus). Residency completed, he returned once more to his home in the Northwest, establishing an office-based practice of psychotherapy and general psychiatry. There, in collaboration with philosopher Thomas Alderson Davis, he began to explore how an understanding of the psychiatric condition "catatonia" may serve as a conceptual anchor for the notion of selfhood; their book *Story by Story: Who I Am, What I Suffer* was a consequence. He had learned from Davis a means for defining enigma, which was the prompt whereby he discovered that a passion for literature and the arts, which had commenced in his childhood, and his thinking about mourning had, in his old age, come together.

SUSAN PICKETT, PHD completed a doctorate early in her career as a musician and began teaching undergraduates music theory and history, as well as coaching the most ambitious string players among them. Yet her self-image for decades, having studied violin performance under John Browning (Sr.), James Buswell, Franco Gulli, and (viola) Virginia Majewski, drew principally on her own musicianship as a soloist and as a and as a chamber player. In her fifties, though, a slowly advancing, pain-laden cervical complication from years of playing prompted a transformation: she launched a new career, one of research into compositions by women forgotten in musical istory. She is now among the leading experts in the world on women composers, through her book on the Bauer sisters, Marion and Emilie Frances; through the three CDs she has created that feature her own performances of women's  music; through her reconstruction from manuscript of Elfrida Andrée's Concert-Ouverture (since performed dozens of times throughout the world); through a feature article about her in the Chronicle of Higher Education; through interviews with her on NPR and on Voice of America; through her personal appearance in a segment about her work on ABC's Good Morning America; and through citations of her research in dissertations, research publications, CD booklets, and encyclopedias. She has, in addition, published three books for instruction in music theory.

MARK G. BROWN, EDD has been a professional musician since his twenties, composing songs and organizing and performing (piano, trumpet, voice) in small bands featured in cities and communities across the nation. Favorite venues have included the Oxford Hotel in Denver, the Sheraton Grand in Los Angeles, and the Main Stage (Bumbershoot Festival) in Seattle. His personal favorites among his song compositions are "Desejandro," "I Will Be There for You," "Same Old Me, Same Old You," and "I'm Coming Home Again." These and others are recorded on five CDs. Songs of his compositions have found a place in two musicals. Brown continues to perform, compose, and record to this very day. In his later thirties, however, prompted by family additions and the still haunting question put to him in his early adulthood by his mother — "What will you do for others?" — he began to pursue the career of a psychotherapist, first earning a master's degree in psychology (Antioch-Seattle), then the EdD degree (Seattle University). He has now practiced psychotherapy for some thirty years.

ACKNOWLEDGMENTS

The late Leigh McCullough inspired this book, unknowingly, as the Introduction will make clear. Another influence of great importance has been that of Salman Akhtar — something apparent from just a quick glance at the References section — though he, too, has been personally unaware that such could be the case, and certainly he should not be saddled with opinions we've come to with which he might disagree.

More directly, we wish to express our gratitude for the personal interest in our project taken by the artist, philosopher, and educator Paul Rotterdam (PhD, University of Vienna, 1966; Lecturer, Harvard University 1966-1987) and by the composer, conductor, and educator Samuel Jones (PhD, University of Rochester 1960; founding dean Shepherd School of Music, Rice University; resident composer Seattle Symphony 1997-2011). The former has written the **Preface** for our book; the latter has written the **Foreword** and devoted hours to poring over the book's details, providing innumerable helpful suggestions along the way. To our readers — Frank Maleson, MD; David Glenn, MM; John David Earnest, MM; Richard Middleton-Kaplan, PhD; and Joseph Wujek, MD — for their comments and support we extend many, many thanks. This work grew from life as a manuscript into life as a book thanks to the experience and expertise of D. Patrick Miller (*https://www.fearlessbooks.com/Literary.html*), to whom we extend our deep gratitude. Kristen Weber (*kweber@ilibribookdesign.com*) has had charge of designing its website and along the way offered additional suggestions pertinent to its availability in the world; for both efforts on our behalf we are thankful. Finally, Mary Bisbee-Beek (*https://www.marybisbeebeek.com*) has served as a Publishing Sherpa indeed, to make use of this title of her own invention, one that's perfectly descriptive — thank you, thank you Mary!

The ideas that underlie this work came together in a single theme for the first time publicly in May 2016. David R. Byrd, MD, professor of surgery, University of Washington School of Medicine, had some months before urged Robert Arnold Johnson to prepare a talk for a particular conference of both professionals and laypersons at the Fred Hutchinson Cancer Center in Seattle. Had Dr. Byrd's prompt not been issued… well, the result is, we'd guess, imponderable, but we are grateful that it was.

www.ingramcontent.com/pod-product-compliance
Lightning Source LLC
Chambersburg PA
CBHW052031030426
42337CB00027B/4959